Cambridge Elements

Elements in Earth System Governance
edited by
Frank Biermann
Utrecht University
Aarti Gupta
Wageningen University
Michael Mason
London School of Economics and Political Science (LSE)

TRANSITION IMAGINARIES

Contested Temporalities, Affective Politics, and Decolonial Technology

Benoit Dillet
University of Bath
Sophia Hatzisavvidou
University of Bath

Shaftesbury Road, Cambridge CB2 8EA, United Kingdom

One Liberty Plaza, 20th Floor, New York, NY 10006, USA

477 Williamstown Road, Port Melbourne, VIC 3207, Australia

314–321, 3rd Floor, Plot 3, Splendor Forum, Jasola District Centre, New Delhi – 110025, India

103 Penang Road, #05–06/07, Visioncrest Commercial, Singapore 238467

Cambridge University Press is part of Cambridge University Press & Assessment, a department of the University of Cambridge.

We share the University's mission to contribute to society through the pursuit of education, learning and research at the highest international levels of excellence.

www.cambridge.org
Information on this title: www.cambridge.org/9781009488785
DOI: 10.1017/9781009488747

© Benoit Dillet and Sophia Hatzisavvidou 2026

This publication is in copyright. Subject to statutory exception and to the provisions of relevant collective licensing agreements, with the exception of the Creative Commons version the link for which is provided below, no reproduction of any part may take place without the written permission of Cambridge University Press & Assessment.

An online version of this work is published at doi.org/10.1017/9781009488747 under a Creative Commons Open Access license CC-BY-NC 4.0 which permits re-use, distribution and reproduction in any medium for non-commercial purposes providing appropriate credit to the original work is given and any changes made are indicated. To view a copy of this license visit https://creativecommons.org/licenses/by-nc/4.0

When citing this work, please include a reference to the DOI 10.1017/9781009488747

First published 2026

A catalogue record for this publication is available from the British Library

ISBN 978-1-009-48878-5 Hardback
ISBN 978-1-009-48875-4 Paperback
ISSN 2631-7818 (online)
ISSN 2631-780X (print)

Cambridge University Press & Assessment has no responsibility for the persistence or accuracy of URLs for external or third-party internet websites referred to in this publication and does not guarantee that any content on such websites is, or will remain, accurate or appropriate.

For EU product safety concerns, contact us at Calle de José Abascal, 56, 1°, 28003 Madrid, Spain, or email eugpsr@cambridge.org

Transition Imaginaries

Contested Temporalities, Affective Politics, and Decolonial Technology

Elements in Earth System Governance

DOI: 10.1017/9781009488747
First published online: January 2026

Benoit Dillet
University of Bath

Sophia Hatzisavvidou
University of Bath

Author for correspondence: Sophia Hatzisavvidou, sh2455@bath.ac.uk

Abstract: The idea that the world needs to transition to a more sustainable future is omnipresent in environmental politics and policy today. Focusing on the energy transition as a solution to the ecological crisis represents a shift in environmental political thought and action. This Element employs a political theory approach and draws on empirical developments to explore this shift by probing the temporal, affective, and technological dimensions of transition politics. Mobilising the framework of ecopolitical imaginaries, it maps five transition imaginaries and sketches a counter-hegemonic, decolonial transition that integrates decolonial approaches to knowledge and technology. *Transition Imaginaries* offers a nuanced exploration of the ways in which transition politics unfolds, and a novel argument on the importance of attending to the coloniality of transition politics. A transition to just sustainable futures requires the mobilisation of post-extractivist visions, knowledges, and technologies. This title is also available as Open Access on Cambridge Core.

Keywords: transition, imaginary, decoloniality, technology, temporality

© Benoit Dillet and Sophia Hatzisavvidou 2026

ISBNs: 9781009488785 (HB), 9781009488754 (PB), 9781009488747 (OC)
ISSNs: 2631-7818 (online), 2631-780X (print)

Contents

1 Introduction 1

2 Transition Politics and the New Conflict of Temporalities 9

3 Ecopolitical Imaginaries of Transition 22

4 The Joyful Transition 39

5 Technology for a Decolonial Transition 51

   References 66

1 Introduction

The idea that we need *a transition* is omnipresent in climate discourses today. Three recent examples illustrate the ubiquitous use of transition in Earth system governance. The first instance occurred at COP28 in Dubai, controversially presided over by Sultan Ahmed Al Jaber, CEO of Abu Dhabi National Oil Co (ADNOC). All parties agreed on a roadmap for 'transitioning away from fossil fuels' (UN, 2023), but no clear timeline was agreed. The second example is the European election campaign in France. Jordan Bardella, the young and media-friendly president of the French far-right party National Rally (RN), announced that France had completed its energy transition (Wakim, 2024). Bardella conflated electricity use (mainly from nuclear energy) with the entire energy consumption mix in a misleading move aiming to defend energy sovereignty. The final example is the Energy Institute (EI) report on the global energy market, which highlights that despite all the rhetoric of green transition, fossil fuel consumption and emissions have reached unprecedented levels. Nick Wayth, Chief Executive of EI, declared 'the transition has not even started' (Chu, 2024). A puzzle, then, emerges: is 'transition' simply a doublespeak for international climate conferences? Has it ended, or has it not even started?

Significant scholarship in political theory and environmental studies has shown how much metaphors and language matter in politics. 'The language of politics is obviously not the language of a single disciplined model of intellectual inquiry,' rightly notes J. G. A. Pollock (1989, p. 17). In politics, the term 'transition' has a long trajectory: it was introduced by international actors who planned large-scale organisational changes conceptualised around the ideas of 'democratic transition' and 'transitional justice'. In climate politics, the term 'transition' is frequently used as a shorthand for 'energy transition', 'ecological transition', or 'green transition'. As discussed in more detail in Section 2, environmental historian Jean-Baptiste Fressoz makes a convincing case for tracing the origin of the S-curve in energy politics from logistics and innovation economics. The political success and purchase of the term 'transition' are fascinating. In this first section, we problematise its polysemic use and prepare the ground for the critical examination of transition imaginaries that follows in the next sections.

A Brief Conceptual Genealogy

Even a cursory investigation into the term 'transition' shows that in the last fifty years, it has been employed to describe or explain social, economic, and political institutional changes. Indeed, the language of transition became central to institutional discourses in the 1990s (Aykut & Evrard, 2017, pp. 18–19). With its focus on the transition to democracy, transitional justice, and transition to a liberal market economy, this paradigm has been popularised by international organisations such as the International Monetary Fund (IMF) and the World Bank, well before the emphasis on energy transition. In the democratisation paradigm, the term 'transition' gave meaning and direction to regime crises and what would otherwise have been a period of deep uncertainty. After the fall of authoritarian regimes in South America and Southern Europe (Portugal, Spain, and Greece) in the 1970s, the democratisation literature flourished with scholars seeking to assess why democratic transitions succeed or fail. After the end of the Cold War, this literature gained a second wind, with (liberal) democracy promoted as the only 'game in town'; armed with analytical and institutional frameworks, scholars attempted to explain the different waves of democratisation and why free trade capitalism was beneficial to democratic regimes (Clary, 2010). During the last two decades, the world has witnessed regime changes, revolutions and restorations, and periods of democratic and authoritarian experimentation, questioning the straightforward narrative of a democratic transition. In attempting to write a history of these transitions, Cristiano Paixão and Massimo Meccarelli (2021, p. 2) note that if transitional justice is understood as 'a single prescription – a uniform set of actions or reparations necessary in a post-dictatorship context', the notion would be either 'somewhat misleading ... [or] almost useless for understanding the numerous processes for the shift from authoritarian regime to constitutional democracy'. Democratisation moves more like a pendulum rather than in waves.

This observation is relevant to the discussion on ecological transitions. Although transitioning to a new, 'green' phase in human history may sound like a novel idea, the vocabulary that permeates the discourse of green transition today has a long history. Indeed, its origins can be found in earlier discourses from the 1950s about demography transition, peak oil, and energy transition (Fressoz, 2024; Smil, 2010).[1] In the 1970s, it gained further traction as the solution to the 'energy crisis', with engineers, industry actors, and politicians in the United States appealing to a phasist energy history. This is

---

[1] Fressoz (2024, pp. 105–110) points out that in politics the term 'transition' was used in socialist circles as a softer and less radical approach to socio-economic regime change than revolution. In the late nineteenth century, George Bernard Shaw (1889) wrote about the 'transition to social democracy' by using a phasist approach; the notion of transition was already mobilised to distinguish the Fabian Society evolutionary socialism from Marxism and communism. Another influential group the Technical Alliance, organised around sociologist Thorstein Veblen, developed in the 1920s and early 1930s new ideas on how to organise the economy in a rational way. The exploitation of machines and the emphasis on energy (rather than dollars) were central to the Technical Alliance.

famously depicted in an 'Address to the Nation on Energy' delivered by Jimmy Carter in 1977:

> Twice in the last several hundred years, there has been a transition in how people use energy. The first was about 200 years ago when we changed away from wood – which had provided about 90 per cent of all fuel – to coal, which was much more efficient. This change became the basis of the Industrial Revolution. The second change occurred in this century, with the growing use of oil and natural gas. (Carter, 1977; also in Fressoz, 2024, p. 262)

The language of 'energy transition' was adopted in 1981 at the United Nations Conference on New and Renewable Sources of Energy in Nairobi and started dominating the global debate about energy (Basosi, 2020). More than forty years later, international politics has widely adopted this language of energy transition to discuss even issues unrelated to the environment and nature. This is captured well in the idea of 'climatisation' of global politics: a condition whereby 'climate change is increasingly becoming the frame of reference for the mediation and hierarchisation of other global issues' (Aykut & Maertens, 2021, p. 502). In high-level policy and governmental responses to the climate crisis, 'transition' refers to the process of achieving a decarbonised world economy. In France, in 2017, under the Macron presidency, the Ministry of the Environment was renamed the Ministry of Ecological Transition; in 2022, a second Department was created, the Ministry of Energy Transition. Similarly, in 2018, the Spanish Ministry of the Environment was renamed the Ministry for the Ecological Transition (and then in 2020, the Ministry for the Ecological Transition and Demographic Challenge). In 2021, at COP26 in Glasgow, the UK Government announced the creation of a Transition Plan Taskforce to develop the gold standard for private sector climate transition plans. This institutionalisation and formalisation of transition in public policy demonstrates the firm grip of the idea on political imagination. Evidently, 'transition' is a shorthand to describe changes in socio-economic systems aiming at low-carbon outcomes.

Academic scholarship on energy transitions has been growing rapidly in the last fifteen years, focusing primarily on socio-technical systems and the innovations required to decarbonise energy production, the cornerstone of the green transition in its mainstream manifestation. A notable concept emerging from the academic and policy debate on low-carbon transitions is 'transition pathways'. This concept 'underscores the multiple directions and processes of low-carbon change; interactions among technological, social, and natural dimensions; and cumulative choices spanning several decades' (Rosenbloom et al., 2019, p. 172). This perspective integrates the literature on path dependence and historical institutionalism to imagine potential low-carbon transitions. The burgeoning field of 'transition studies' – led by scholars such as Frank W. Geels, Peter Newell and Benjamin K. Sovacool (Geels et al., 2017) – focuses primarily on innovation and technological adoption. Using a complex lexicon to convey different scenarios and adjust parameters, these contributions take the discussion on the transition to a high level of abstraction (Fressoz, 2024, pp. 29–30).[2] As Avelino (2017) notes, power is frequently undervalued in the sustainability transitions literature, treating it instrumentally rather than an end in itself; yet, analysing power relations can help to approach critically the contradictions inherent in transition processes.

Another concept that has gained traction in agendas and practices of organisations on every level of governance today is the idea of 'just transitions'. Grasped initially as a response to the resurgence of neoliberal globalisation calling to treat workers and communities affected by transitions in a just way, the just transition framework is multifaceted, covering different breadths, depths, and ambitions (Stevis, 2023). As a result, just transition is also highly contested as a framework for not addressing socioeconomic and environmental inequities. Stefania Barca (2020, p. 50) shows that the just transition framework reflects 'a masculinist and Western-centric bias that persists in most large trade union confederations (even when women lead them), focusing on blue-collar jobs in heavy industry and infrastructures as the only sectors worth defending and "greening", while downplaying the crucial contribution of agriculture, domestic and social reproduction work'. As Stevis (2023, p. 59) clarifies, promises to 'not leave anyone behind' can obscure the politics of systemic change and blur the importance of local campaigns and struggles.

Another interesting manifestation of the term can be identified in the successful and well-known grassroots initiative of Transition Towns, which also contributed to the popularisation of the term in civil society. This citizen-led movement mainly focuses on energy independence, small-scale agriculture, and local food production. Co-founded in Totnes (UK) in 2007 by Rob Hopkins, an experienced permaculture teacher, and his former students Louise Rooney and Catherine Dunne, the Transition Network is a charity that aims to roll out transition principles to other towns around the UK and the world. Within a few years, the movement resulted in hundreds of hubs worldwide, thus challenging the idea of citizen apathy given climate change (North, 2010; Urry, 2011). The extraordinary spread of the movement can be attributed to its simple message of reclaiming

---

[2] For instance, in a 2017 issue of *Science*, we read: 'we present a "sociotechnical" framework to address the multi-dimensionality of the deep decarbonization challenge and show how coevolutionary interactions between technologies and societal groups can accelerate low-carbon transitions' (Geels et al., 2017).

community, skills, and resourcefulness. This message found fertile ground in the austerity conditions that the 2008 financial crisis created (Hopkins & Astruc, 2017). Transition Towns played an instrumental role in filling gaps in local services due to local authorities' shrinking budgets following the 2008–2015 governmental austerity policies. Nonetheless, its emphasis on resilience bizarrely resonated with the austerity message of the 'big society' and the role played by volunteering in the collapse of the welfare state (Smith & Jones, 2015). In any case, the movement's use of the term 'transition' played a role in popularising (and localising) the notion that a socio-ecological transition is needed, making it central to local politics and citizen activism.

Overall, we observe that in its current use, whether referring to energy, sustainability, low-carbon, or socio-ecological transformations, 'transition' denotes a *temporal* and *qualitative* movement towards a greener future condition. Underpinning the term is a narrative that seeks to describe and evaluate our present moment: change is ongoing, and a new phase that is more ecologically sound will be reached. Transition is, therefore, a future-oriented term that seeks to define our contemporary condition as one in which everyone and everything should be mobilised in this journey towards genuine sustainability.

Contribution

The idea of transition is prominent in the Earth system governance scholarship on the planetary (Stevis & Felli, 2020), national (Morena et al., 2018), and local (Berglund et al., 2023) levels. This Element contributes to this flourishing field from a political theory perspective. Political theorists have made rich contributions to our understanding of the state's role in ecological transitions (Eckersley, 2021; Hatzisavvidou, 2020), how sovereignty changes with a changing climate (Mann & Wainwright, 2018), and the importance of expanding the concept of justice that underpins Earth system governance towards a direction that integrates more-than-human-natures (Celermajer et al., 2025). We contend that a political theory perspective on the study of transition politics can illuminate the conceptual and ideological pluralism that characterises this domain of politics by attending simultaneously to its normative and empirical aspects.

The starting point of this investigation is acknowledging that the idea of transition is used in polysemic ways. Behind the semblance of agreement are competing politics and power grab in the name of transition. To dispel misunderstandings, we do not reject the macropolitical project of the green transition or the energy transition. Like other critical transition studies scholars (Rosenbloom & Meadowcroft, 2022; Sovacool, 2021), we are interested in the effects of pursuing transition politics. Scholars such as Smil, Sovacool, and others frequently criticise transition based on the length of transition processes; these critics identify the problem with the transition's technological and economic complexity, which prevents more rapid changes. Our approach differs in three ways. First, we do not critique the speed of transition but rather the epistemology that underpins the dominant transition vision and the politics through which it is advanced. Our project is a political theory of transition politics that draws on empirical developments to attend to the green transition's ontological, epistemological, and cognitive aspects. Second, unlike scholars in transition studies who focus on the 'meso-level' of analysis (Köhler et al., 2019), namely that of socio-technical systems, we are concerned with the 'macro-level', the level where systemic changes are required. Third, we are interested in critically probing different transition visions. Even though the idea of transition is ubiquitous today in political rhetoric and the vocabulary of social organisations, businesses, and governments, we observe that there are different ways in which transitions to low-carbon futures are envisioned. This critical approach dispels the myth that environmental politics is a 'valence issue', namely an issue on which there is broad public agreement about desired policy outcomes and that, therefore, it is beyond contestation and disagreement. In developing a political theory of transition politics, we look at four elements: temporal and historical experiences of transitions, ecopolitical imaginaries of transitions, the affective dimension of transitions and finally, a decolonial transition that centres decolonial technology.

This Element has two aims. The first aim of *Transition Imaginaries* is to unearth the historical, normative, and political consequences deriving from using the green transition as a central tenet of climate politics. We demonstrate that the faith in 'progress' that permeates the mainstream transition vision harbours a form of delayism – the continuous postponement of meaningful socio-ecological change. Using materialist environmental history, we examine the assumptions that underpin and sustain the dominant transition narrative. We show that the attempt to mobilise people, materials, energies, and natures in the journey towards 'real sustainability' perpetuates the logic that informs what Walter Mignolo (2011) calls 'the colonial matrix of power'. The second aim is to highlight the role of ecopolitical imaginaries in organising how transition is envisaged and advanced. Imaginaries are powerful political motifs, as political actors use them to produce shared meanings about the world, using cognitive schemes, cultural artefacts, metaphors, and narratives. Ecopolitical imaginaries also produce positive and negative affects, a vital issue we discuss at length in this Element.

Our overarching argument is that the currently hegemonic manifestation of transition politics is damaging in a triple sense: first, it hinders the realisation of forms of ecological politics that draw on marginalised philosophies of history and conceptions of time; second, it contributes to the development of sad affects through a disengaging technocratic and business-as-usual approach; and third, it results in further environmental damage in the present in the name of a greener future. Transition is a term often mobilised as the leading solution to the climate emergency; as such, it can function as a consensual term that depoliticises and smoothens forms of contestation. We concur with other scholars that a socio-ecological transition is imperative to ensure a sustainable and just future for everyone and everything. Our critique concerns the dominant transition paradigm rather than the idea of transition per se. The transition imaginaries we identify and analyse are the outcome of theoretical engagement with the unfolding conflicts we observe today in rhetoric, practices, and socio-material relations. Rather than systematically analysing transition plans and programmes, we offer a critical account of transition imaginaries.

This Element contributes to the current scholarship on Anthropocene politics and contemporary political theory more broadly by dissecting the variants of transition politics; highlighting the new conflict of temporalities; attending to the affective dimensions of the green transition; de-centring the role played by technological innovation. The Element, then, contributes to four contextual conditions of the Earth System Governance Research Framework (Earth System Governance Project, 2018, p. 48) – transformations, inequalities, Anthropocene, and diversity – by engaging with the current transition imaginaries as well as providing an alternative conceptualisation of transition, informed by a more diverse understanding of technology and temporality as well as marginalised forms of knowledge. The combination of our critical and decolonial approach builds on the diversity of the epistemological orientations of the ESG Research Framework (Earth System Governance Project, 2018, p. 38) to encompass views and cosmologies that go beyond Eurocentric accounts of knowledge production.

Outline

This Element is organised into four sections. In Section 2, we build on the work of the French environmental historian Jean-Baptiste Fressoz (2024) and his genealogy of energy transition to examine the origins of the transition narrative. We take this idea further and argue that the vision of a post-carbon future reverberates both as a temporal order and as a knowledge system. Transition can be defined as 'a black box that lies between the present and our idealised visions of the future' (Heron & Dean, 2022). This concept presents the temporal order of climate politics as brighter and linear, building from the modern regime of historicity (Hartog, 2015). This section concludes that the climate emergency has produced a new conflict of temporalities and historical experience.

Section 3 employs the notion of ecopolitical imaginary to dissect the ideological underpinnings and empirical manifestations of transition politics. Although it is undeniable that, in the descriptive sense, we are amid an unfolding transition to a planetary age, it is also crucial that the nuances and unequal outcomes of this process are also understood and interpreted in normative ways. To achieve this, we sketch five ecopolitical imaginaries through which transition politics gains cogency today: technocapitalist, eco-authoritarian, ecosocialist, post-growth, and ecoanarchist. We aim to demonstrate the ubiquity of transition politics while offering a nuanced analysis of its different manifestations and the damaging and beneficial effects produced on intellectual, affective, and material levels.

Section 4 draws on affective approaches to politics to explore and understand the epidemic of eco-anxiety today. Having examined transition imaginaries in Section 3, this section shows how affective attachments constitute and derive from an imaginary. The current preoccupation with the future, in terms of the sixth mass extinction or post-apocalyptic futures, produces sad affects such as eco-anxiety and grief. These sad affects diminish our power to act by dissociating people from the climate issue. Considering the ability of affects to augment or diminish our power to act, we point to the importance of infusing any alternative to the dominant transition paradigm with positive affects, such as joy and pleasure. We discuss the local experimentations of ZAD Notre-Dame-des-Landes as offering new positive attachments that counter the technocapitalist transition imaginary. We analyse these local experimentations as producers of joyful affects. Rather than serving as models of a utopian living, they function as images and produce affects, connecting to the structural and collective order.

Section 5 fleshes out the argument for a decolonial transition by focusing on the question of technology. We return to questions of temporality discussed in Section 1 and challenge the association of technology with anticipation. In the last section, we recover alternative conceptions of technology that exist today to displace the transition imaginary's focus away from technologies typically associated with the dominant transition imaginary. In doing so, we turn to Bernard Stiegler's philosophical work to sharpen our understanding of technology, its place in climate politics and its possible uses. Technology is often hailed as the ultimate and fitting solution to environmental degradation, energy systems, and sustainable living. We argue that there is no escape from technology; global climate change is a technological matter through and through. To show the problem of conceptualisation of technology, we turn to decolonial approaches to technology and two notable examples: the complex vernacular water harvesting techniques in Rajasthan, India, and the restoration of riverscapes by US environmental groups mimicking beaver dam activities. We conclude by sketching a decolonial transition imaginary.

2 Transition Politics and the New Conflict of Temporalities

The idea of a transition to a low-carbon future is ubiquitous in politics and public policy today, steering decision-making, industrial strategy, and financial investment towards solutions and projects that can contribute to implementing this ambitious idea. Three recent examples illustrate this omnipresence of transition in ecopolitics today: the European Green Deal (2020), Biden's Green Industrial Policy (2022), and China's 14th Five-Year Plan (2020). Notwithstanding their differences in objectives, mechanisms, and deadlines, all these transition plans (which account for over half of the world economy) explicitly state a commitment to a single overarching goal: economic growth via a green transition.[3] On the national level, and in alignment with the Paris Agreement (2015), which introduced the goal to keep global warming well below 2°C above pre-industrial levels, these plans reflect a 'new' growth strategy that aims to spur long-term economic growth fuelled by renewable energy sources. On the international level, not unlike the idea of 'sustainable development' (WCED, 1987), the green transition is today advanced as a universal goal that both the affluent Global North and the dispossessed Global South can pursue. In this sense, transition is a large-scale, universal project that attempts to speak to the needs and interests of all countries, irrespective of their past and present conditions.

The idea of a shared vision for humanity fits an era branded as the Anthropocene, the epoch of humans. What originally started as a debate between geologists very quickly captured the imagination of researchers in humanities and social sciences and even attained a broader cultural and political significance (Malhi, 2017). Although the diagnosis that it is the unifying category of *anthropos* that caused this change remains widely contested (see especially Bonneuil and Fressoz 2016; Haraway 2015; Moore 2015), the advent of the Anthropocene on the conceptual and analytical levels marks an opportunity to reconsider the relationship between humanity and nature. As an event highlighting human-induced processes on the Earth, the Anthropocene creates opportunities for reflecting and acting upon the past and how human interventions, successes, and mistakes have shaped it. To

---

[3] The second Trump administration dismantled federal climate mitigation and adaptation measures, including pausing funding for Inflation Reduction Act (IRA). Nonetheless, at the time of writing, scholars and commentators agree that the clean energy transition is well underway.

the extent that modern ways of thinking have primarily informed such interventions, the Anthropocene marks an opportunity to reckon with them, to reconsider, confront, and revise them. It, therefore, calls into attention questions around epistemic injustice, the privileging of certain cosmologies over others, and the expropriation of earth materials in unequal and damaging ways.

Nonetheless, unproblematically advancing a concrete, monolithic vision for a green transition as a new common goal that 'humanity' – an undifferentiated agent that has collectively altered the Earth system – can jointly pursue overlooks these critical questions. Crucially, it misses the opportunity to reflect on the past and to respond to the injustices that marked it, with damaging effects manifesting in the present and anticipated in the future. The political use of transition is 'ambivalent' since it emphasises both the necessity of change and circumscriptions to protect the current political regime (Aykut & Evrard, 2017, p. 19). Notably, the transition is, first and foremost, an argument about ordering time. As a political idea, it is underpinned by a particular understanding of temporality and our experience of it as humans via history. Yet, the transition also obscures the dramatic shift in historical experience; with the Anthropocene, there is an awareness of diachronicity and conflict of temporalities: the past, present and future are no longer organised according to the modern regime of historicity. As Andreas Malm (2018, p. 11) explains,

> There is no synchronicity in climate change. Now more than ever, we inhabit the diachronic, the discordant, the inchoate: the fossil fuels hundreds of millions of years old, the mass combustion developed over the past two centuries, the extreme weather this has already generated, the journey towards a future that will be infinitely more extreme – unless something is done now – the tail of present emissions stretching into the distance ... History has sprung alive through a nature that has done likewise.

Climate change results from deliberate, unjust, colonial, and criminal actions in the past. In the Anthropocene, the past is ever-present in the present; past actions haunt damaged and ruined landscapes. The future is either in peril or envisioned as a utopian territory composed of sustainable practices supported by green technologies.

Transition as a Hegemonic Idea

The idea of 'transition' as a policy, social, and economic goal is prevalent across different intellectual and political circles today; it is *hegemonic*. In this section, we outline this project's origins and what it entails for the understanding of temporality in climate politics. Hegemony refers to the process and outcome of a social bloc's efforts to secure domination and authority by integrating the interests of other social forces through a combination of consent and coercion (Gramsci, 1971; Hall, 1988). We purposefully use 'hegemony' here to call to attention the fact that what we discuss as green transition refers to the specific form that transition politics has taken today as a policy paradigm. Despite the semblance of agreement on the idea of a transition to a low-carbon future, this hegemony is contested by other ecopolitical imaginaries (Sections 3 and 5). On the international policymaking level, the green transition is presented as a strategic set of policy instruments that aim to curtail carbon emissions fast enough to prevent global temperatures from transgressing the dangerous threshold of 2°C above pre-industrial levels.[4] With the horizon of action to achieve this goal set until 2050 or 2060, the green transition includes ambitious plans to decarbonise all aspects of economic activity in energy, land use, industry, buildings, and transport. A central characteristic of the transition as a hegemonic idea is what Breno Bringel and Maristella Svampa (2023) call the 'decarbonisation consensus': a 'new global agreement' that promotes a carbon-free energy system based on electrification and digitisation and contributes to the exacerbation of environmental destruction and socioeconomic inequalities. In addition to this decarbonisation consensus, the green transition expresses a particular way of getting there. It implies thinking about temporality, history, and the role of humans as agents of all change on Earth. Bringing together the dominant Western-centred cosmology and the systems of knowledge associated with it, along with the institutional power accumulated on the level of global governance of the Earth system, the vision of a transition to a low-carbon world is projected as a widely accepted, jointly pursued goal.

Seemingly, the aspiration is to transform all aspects of social life radically towards more sustainable directions; in reality, the green transition is, first and foremost, an example of the economisation of life, a process theorised and well documented by Murphy (2017). Take the example of the EU Green Deal. This ambitious policy package aspires to 'transform the EU into a modern, resource-efficient and competitive economy' in which 'economic growth is decoupled from resource use' while 'reducing net greenhouse gas emissions by at least 55% by 2030, compared to 1990 levels', ultimately ensuring that by 2050 there will be no net emissions of greenhouse gases (Murphy, 2017). Although it is presented as a holistic plan aiming to transform all domains of human activity

---

[4] In 2018 the Intergovernmental Panel for Climate Change (the United Nations body for assessing the science related to climate change) published a Special Report that revised this threshold to 1.5°C, explaining that 'climate-related risks for natural and human systems are higher for global warming of 1.5°C than at present, but lower than at 2°C' (IPCC, 2018). Despite the fact that the report received a lot of public attention, supported by bold news headlines, public policymaking and implementation maintains the 2°C goal as more attuned to the realities of the global economic system.

and nature (air, soil, water, and biodiversity), the Green Deal is primarily a policy package to transition to a carbon-neutral *economy*. This is evidenced by the kind of directives, mechanisms, and instruments through which the Green Deal is delivered.

Yet, its proponents mobilise arguments beyond the economic sphere to acquire a hegemonic status and coalesce different social forces around the green transition. This is why the green transition is frequently presented as a social programme that aims to 'improve the well-being and health of citizens and future generations' (EU Green Deal) and to be 'the largest investment ever in combatting the existential crisis of climate change' while lowering prescription drug costs, health care costs, and energy costs (US Inflation Reduction Act). It is a vision for an improved society where everyone can reap the benefits of the growing economy. Advanced through 'win-win' rhetoric, which presents a particular form of transition to a low-carbon economy as the most beneficial scenario for our climate-changed world, the idea of transition has taken up most of the space of ecological politics on the public policy level in many of the world's largest economies. Despite its seemingly novel, neutral, and consensual character, the green transition is the latest addition to the grand narratives of progress, development, and growth (Escobar, 2015; Kothari et al., 2019). These three processes have marked the history of modernity comprising the goal of what Walter D. Mignolo (2011) calls 'the colonial matrix of power': a structure that, in reality, includes not only these goals but also coloniality, manifesting through poverty, injustices, and corruption. The reality of *climate coloniality* is today unfolding 'where Eurocentric hegemony, neocolonialism, racial capitalism, uneven consumption, and military domination are co-constitutive of climate impacts experienced by variously racialised populations who are disproportionately made vulnerable and disposable' (Sultana, 2022, p. 4).

It is essential to acknowledge that the idea of an energy transition is not novel; it is well embedded within a broader narrative of humanity's common journey on Earth. It is even composed of smaller competing narratives upheld by different public actors that emphasise either sustainable energy or decarbonised energy (therefore including nuclear energy) (Aykut & Evrard, 2017, p. 31). Low-carbon transformations require investments over generations, and historical studies are crucial to understanding the weight of history in politics. While the genealogy of transition as an idea does not predetermine its current manifestations in governmental policy, political actors constantly mobilise history, as demonstrated by Fressoz and others. In his last book, environmental historian Jean-Baptiste Fressoz examines the origin of the energy transition in the post-WWII United States to understand why it has become a dominant frame of reference in different domains of politics and not just in environmental policies.

Fressoz's genealogy of the concept of 'energy transition' finds that the timeline of the transition narrative follows 'a "phasist" perception of energy' (Fressoz, 2022, p. 116). According to this logic, the history of energy production and consumption is represented as a series of phases and transitions. More specifically, in the 1950s and 1960s, the narrators of these transition 'histories' appealed to common sense and naturalised transitions. They argued that humanity had already experienced two transitions: from wood to coal and from coal to oil. The point was to prepare for the next transition: from oil to nuclear energy. Fressoz shows the limitations of this phasist interpretation of the history of energy production and consumption. He contends that we should shift perspective: from a phasist understanding of the history of energy (and its focus on 'transition') to an accumulative understanding (Fressoz, 2020).[5] As he explains, historically, 'sources of energy are as much part of a symbiosis as a competition' (Fressoz, 2022, p. 116). For instance, the 'transition' from wood to coal involved more global wood use (in coal extraction). Similarly, coal consumption increased only when oil became a central energy source for industrialised economies, necessitating new networks to enable oil extraction, refinement, transportation, and distribution. An *accumulative* interpretation of the history of energy, rather than a phasist one, emphasises *dynamic* understanding of past transformations rather than mere transitions. This shift from viewing history of matter as a succession of material phases to a more complex process whereby different intellectual, material, and political forces intermesh opens the way for a comprehensive understanding of transition. Knowledge and material production are more interconnected than a phasist historiography allows it. An approach that considers both the material and the intellectual aspects underpinning the green transition illuminates how it guides ecopolitical decisions and practices today, leading to a delayed meaningful action. Additionally, such an integrated approach encourages the consideration of the devastating impacts of the green transition on racialised and impoverished people and their ecosystems. As Cara New Daggett (2018) notes, energy and work have always been intertwined, and the green transition attempts to conceal the power dynamics inherent in energy production and consumption.

Fressoz's genealogy shows that the energy transition is neither historically novel nor intellectually groundbreaking. Its origins can be traced back to various

---

[5] Other studies support Fressoz's claim. For instance, Richard York and Shannon Bell (2019) suggests using the expression 'energy additions' rather than 'energy transitions'. They write: 'calling the addition of renewables to the energy supply an "energy *transition*" may not only be misleading, but also potentially counter-productive, as such claims may provide the false impression of imminent reductions in carbon emissions and thereby suppress efforts to bring about a genuine transition *away from* fossil fuels' (York and Bell, 2019, p. 41). In his review, Adam Tooze (2025) refers to On Barak's 2020 *Powering Empire* as anticipating Fressoz's argument.

sources: the atomic energy lobby, neo-Malthusians concerned about birth control, the influential 'peak oil' hypothesis, and the application of the logistic model (or S-curve) to the evolution of global energy mix. The energy transition narrative is a patchwork of disparate futurologies, each presenting a unique perspective on the future. These perspectives are driven by a commitment to preventing a catastrophe (a fossil fuel-free future). Fressoz concludes that in reusing and reproducing this transition framework in response to the current ecological crisis, we are perpetuating a 'fake history built on recomforting illusion' of energy transition and a 'phantom future' (Fressoz, 2022, p. 145).

Fressoz's arguments will likely be debated for years to come, and some early criticisms and correctives are worth noting. For instance, Adam Tooze (2025) rightly notes that Fressoz's genealogy remains centred around Anglo-American economies and neglects the significant rise in global emissions from East Asian economies from the 1990s, mainly due to the prominence of steel production and shipbuilding. Pierre Charbonnier (2024) expresses concerns about the normative implications of Fressoz's laser-sharp empirical work in crafting a properly materialist history of energy. The book's ambiguities lie in its lack of discussion of degrowth as an alternative path to the green transition, which Charbonnier suggests could lead to resignation or fatalism in the face of the magnitude of the climate emergency. This sentiment was echoed by a collective of social scientists writing in *Le Monde* shortly after the book's release (Creti et al., 2024). As with any book, interpretations and receptions vary, highlighting the significance of Fressoz's ideas and the need to expand upon them. Fressoz's sobering perspective on the absence of an actual transition can indeed be read in a pessimistic and anxiety-inducing way, a point we delve into in greater detail in Section 4.

Building on Fressoz's conclusion, we extend the discussion beyond energy transitions to encompass transition politics. This involves forms of collective organisation and arrangement of bodies, materials, and natures necessary for transitioning to a decarbonised future. We argue that the post-carbon narrative, which is one of the transition narratives (Aykut & Evrard, 2017), manifests as a philosophy of history (as a way of understanding history) and as a politics (a way of organising societies and natures) through which transition is materialised. We discuss these in turn next: taken together, these two components illuminate the multiple layers to which the idea of transition manifests and can be linked.

The Temporal Order of Transition

While the histories of energy transitions are materially inaccurate, they still have socio-political effects. Reinhardt Koselleck's concept of historical experience provides insight into how the idea of green transition has shaped how humans experience temporality. Koselleck (2018) explains that a defining characteristic of modernity was the acceleration of human time perception, which was associated with the invention of clocks and railways. This acceleration led to the 'denaturalisation of time' (Koselleck, 2018, p. 82; 85–91); as transportation became no longer limited by human or horsepower, or even wind and rain, but rather amplified greatly by machines and steam power. With modernity, the articulation of past, present, and future changed, driven by an impatience for progress and revolution. We observe that the ecological crisis has now opened a new conflict of temporalities, pitting human temporality against geological time, also known 'anthropocenic time', 'climate change temporality' (Simon & Tamm, 2023), or 'deep time' (Hanusch, 2024). These different terminologies mobilised by authors include different parameters and scopes, primarily focusing on biophysical processes or incorporating human experience.

The paradox of transition politics lies in its ability to mobilise a modern experience of time for a historical period where revolution and progress are no longer operative as historical categories. This historical period is often characterised as 'presentism' (Hartog, 2015), a long and repetitive experience of the now. The Anthropocene and the recent large-scale collective consciousness of the climate crisis have disrupted the modern 'regime of historicity', giving rise to a new one, the anthropocenic or climate change temporalities (Nordbland, 2021). In the modern regime of historicity, the future appeared as a *telos*, and the idea of progress became central, providing justification for various doctrines, both eschatological and secular. The Age of Reason and Enlightenment, along with scientific discoveries and modern science, were powerful motifs that reinforced this modern regime of historicity. As Hartog explains, the concept of 'presentism' accounts for the transformation of historical experience caused by the fall of the Berlin Wall in 1989 and the end of the USSR. With the end of the real-existing communism, people's experience of political and historical alternatives vanished, and the present became the immanent and limitless reservoir of historical experience. Real-existing capitalism constructed the regime of 'presentism', the temporality of capital that seeks to subsume all forms of life and temporalities.

In recognising the existence of climate change and the role of humans as a geological force, a new conflict of temporalities and historical experience has emerged. Although Hartog considers the emergence of an ecological consciousness in terms of the regime of historicity, he hesitates to give it a new name. He uses the expression 'apocalypse in slow motion' (Hartog, 2022, p. 82) to conceptualise the reconfiguration of the past-present-future schema in the age of the climate crisis. The recent rise of eco-anxiety (Section 4) is partly linked to this new conflict of temporalities:

> There is fear at times that are approaching too fast (the looming prospect of tipping points), and deep frustration at other times that are both too short and too slow (the short-termism and political delays of electoral democracy); there is sadness and nostalgia at times that are now out of reach (the future is already gone). (Knops, 2023, p. 203)

We concur with Louise Knops that the perception of the looming tipping points is central to this new regime of historicity. Unlike the modern regime of historicity that hailed the future as a brighter and more prosperous period to come, the 'apocalypse in slow motion' represents a new form of shared historical experience in which the present effectively burns the future. Unlike presentism, in which the future is a mere continuation of the limitless present, in the Anthropocenic regime of historicity, a new and negative image of the future emerges. The future is not only worse than the present, but it is deteriorating even more. The unfolding of the biodiversity extinction and the extreme weather systems feed this image of a burning future. There are different ways of describing this new form of historical experience. Some talk about 'pre-traumatic stress syndrome' (Kaplan, 2020; Mihai & Thaler, 2023), a fear of a future event that is already causing wounds in the present. Contrary to other environmental mental health disorders, such as ecosickness or ecophobia, pre-traumatic stress syndrome is a temporal notion based on an anticipation of a catastrophic future, partly created and sustained by dystopian films and fiction.

Interestingly, transition belongs to the modern regime of historicity, one in which the future gives sense to both the past and the present. Transition denotes a dynamic process with specific temporal and qualitative connotations, designating a shift from a carbon-intensive present towards a decarbonised, healthier, or, in other ways, improved future. Indeed, it affirms and validates change as a linear process: a more ecologically sound phase will be reached in the future if appropriate action is taken in the present. The temporal order underpinning transition defines the contemporary condition in a way that seeks to mobilise people, materials, energies, and natures in the journey towards 'real sustainability' with two effects: first, it perpetuates the logic of coloniality that informs the colonial matrix of power; second, it generates a 'passive present' (Danowski & De Castro, 2017) thus foreclosing political possibilities and creating negative affects. As a future-oriented process, transition draws on linear perceptions of time advanced by settler colonialism and the forms of knowledge it privileges (Rifkin, 2017). In this sense, the transition vision shares epistemological ground with the Western-centric understanding of modernity produced in an exploitative centre (Europe) that prospered by impoverishing an abundant periphery (Global South) on both material and cognitive levels. In sharing this ground, the transition vision reproduces the epistemic injustices that characterise the system of knowledge that Mignolo (2011) calls 'the Western code', which was advanced through the colonisation not only of lands but also of time:

> 'time' is a fundamental concept in building the imaginary of the modern/colonial world and an instrument for both controlling knowledge and advancing a vision of society based on progress and development. (Mignolo, 2011, p. 163)

The implementation and success of modernity and its associated economic, political, and social projects required the moulding of time. The ecological crisis is yet another instance in history when time is controlled not only in the name of progress, development, and growth as has been historically done, but also in the name of human civilisation's survival. It is, therefore, not sufficient to examine transition politics as a mere continuation of the project of modernity. The phasist dimension of transition renews the project of modernity itself.

This is why it matters how the idea of a transition to a low-carbon future is narrated: what temporal orders are employed (a topic discussed in this section), what kind of imaginaries arise within it (a topic we discuss in the next section), who is seen as the agent of history driving this transition, and what are the material and affective impacts that this transition has (topics discussed throughout this Element). At stake on the intellectual level here is avoiding the repetition of a mistake that those who have narrated similar stories in the past have made: failing to consider the biophysical state of the Earth system. This mistake was explained in an exchange between Bruno Latour and Dipesh Chakrabarty, who discussed how predominant philosophies of history have traditionally overlooked the role of the Earth system as an agent of history. Latour proposes that historians studying the present have failed to account for the role of the Earth in human history due to an 'excess of "moral clarity"'. This resulted in philosophies of history that were 'blind themselves by the idea of a *goal-oriented* history', which in turn 'has triggered a form of (in)voluntary ignorance about the real state of the Earth' (Latour & Chakrabarty, 2020, pp. 423–427).[6] Latour's diagnosis is invaluable because it makes blatantly clear the fact that although the first signs of the ecological crisis were already evident from the 1980s, modernist philosophies of history failed to account for it.

---

[6] 'It's most likely that having a philosophy of history is a pose; that there is nothing so grandiose in the march of time and certainly nothing like some call for humans to realize a plan, a *telos*, a drive toward some Omega Point' (Latour in Chakrabarty & Latour, 2020, p. 426).

Equally invaluable, though, is Chakrabarty's counterargument: it was not an excess of 'moral clarity' of the West that prevented historians from grasping what he calls 'the planetary' (the equivalent to Latour's Gaia) in human history. As Chakrabarty explains (Latour & Chakrabarty, 2020, p. 451), 'postcolonial thought – for all its critique of the nation-state and race-class formations – was also just as environmentally blind as anti-colonial nationalism.' For Chakrabarty, the planetary became the blind spot of historians because of the dividing line separating postcolonial thinkers and those embedded in Western epistemologies and ontologies, which entails that they have been preoccupied with different problems and questions. This lack of common ground can be remedied – albeit only in a patchy way using 'band-aids' as he suggests – if geological time is brought into historical time. This would entail considering the Anthropocene not simply as a geological process but as an epoch that forces a novel process of historicisation that bridges the hitherto distinct regions of knowledge, philosophy of history and philosophy of nature.

The idea that the green transition is the definitive action that will insulate humanity from the vicissitudes that the advent of the Anthropocene brings by ensuring that an ecological catastrophe will be averted exemplifies *the kind of philosophy of history* critically discussed by Latour and Chakrabarty. As an attempt to organise disparate events into a coherent whole and narrate them as a teleological story, it is a repetition of the mistake identified in their critical exchange. Despite seemingly an attempt to fold 'the planetary' into human attempts to govern nature, the green transition narrative functions as a grand narrative of human progress that advances towards a firmly defined *telos* (a decarbonised society); it thus displays the shortcomings of all philosophies of history identified by Latour. Mistaken by 'the idea of a goal-oriented history' (Latour & Chakrabarty, 2020, p. 427), the green transition vision ignores the reality of biophysical limits, advancing 'technofixes' that, if pursued at the proposed scale, would contribute to the transgression of critical planetary boundaries (International Energy Agency 2022; Dillet & Hatzisavvidou, 2022). This mistake also leaves the idea of transition insensitive to the vicissitudes of those who are called to shoulder the environmental, health, and social costs of the extraction projects linked to transition, an aspect that we discuss more fully next. With its emphasis on a future affirmed as a horizon of anticipation, an endpoint that humanity as a unified agent marches towards, the idea of transition not only misses the geospatial dimension that Latour and Chakrabarty's exchange illuminates but also fails to pay attention to the pluralism of temporalities embraced by different societies and communities that are called to endorse and pursue the transition vision.

In contrast to this discussion, in Section 5, we turn to decolonial approaches to technology and time as alternatives to the dominant and modernist transition narrative. Indeed, not everyone in the world lives or aspires to live in the same temporality. Drawing from his work on and with the Zapatistas in Mexico, Jérôme Baschet (2022, p. 201) shows the significance of cyclical temporality of the indigenous communities alongside the modern and presentist regimes of temporality. In engaging with alternative understandings of temporality, we illuminate how counter-hegemonic views of time and technology also point to alternative transition imaginaries.

Transition Politics

The temporal order that infuses and sustains the dominant transition imaginary offers a one-sided, uniform, and totalising account of human history in the era of unprecedented anthropogenic climate change. When the temporal logic of transition is placed within a broader epistemological context, the green transition is an episode in the long history of modernity and the colonial matrix power. Functioning through a series of coordinated actions that resulted in yet-to-be-repaired epistemic injustices, the cognitive empire invaded the mental universe of the colonised, framing their ontological commitments and colonising their epistemological processes in ways that enabled capitalist extractivist and political subordination (Ndlovu-Gatsheni, 2021).[7] As argued in Mignolo's quote earlier, time was a key reference point in the process of colonising people's mental and affective processes; it was also central in the re-organisation of life around markets, money, and 'the economy', a re-organisation that required not only a way to measure and evaluate time but also the homogenisation of time so that it could be used as a resource.

In its dominant conceptualisation, the green transition is organised in a homogenous temporal framework that overwrites any differing way of appreciating time, thus erasing the pluralism of existing temporalities from policy planning. This is patently clear in the transition plans through which transition politics gains cogency. This is a politics comprising a series of practices, such as legislations, policies, and investments that aim at implementing the transition to a decarbonised society and economy within a specified timeframe – 2030 (e.g. EU), 2050 (e.g. the United States), or 2060 (e.g. China), depending on the ambition and perceived responsibility of each climate actor. Even in its most statist and bureaucratised version as 'ecological planning', the idea that the

---

[7] This is not to argue that all visions for 'soft', 'renewable', and 'clean' energy paths are part of the colonial project. Rather, the claim here is that the way that the green transition today unfolds advances extractivism and homogenises epistemologies.

future can be constructed remains central. These sets of practices make up transition politics, the essence of which is exhausted in achieving 'carbon neutrality' by the set timescale at all costs. Although the transition timescales carry the authority of science, as they are the product of complex, collaborative research practices, they are far from 'neutral' or 'objective' depictions of reality. As important work in science and technology studies shows, time is co-produced with social arrangements, political order, and technoscientific advances (Marquardt & Delina, 2021). The timescales of decarbonisation are not simply the outcome of powerful calculations by neutral computer models; they reflect political and economic priorities, deep ideological commitments, and funding choices. They integrate, in other words, views on what kind of knowledge matters and what kind of social and economic orders are envisioned. *Transition politics is a mechanism for organising societies, natures, affects, and resources in the present so that the Earth's atmosphere contains fewer greenhouse gases in the future.* It is a future-oriented politics that, in its unfolding, may cause irreparable damage to landscapes and historically marginalised, impoverished, and racialised communities through extraction and homogenisation. To prevent this damage, transition politics should take a justice approach, a variant of which we outline in Section 5.

In its currently hegemonic manifestation, transition politics takes the form of ambient Prometheanism, the doctrine that 'advocates humanity's ability to confront the ecological crisis through costly technological interventions fuelled by intensified economisation' (Dillet & Hatzisavvidou, 2022, 352). By centring all environmental action around 'carbon neutrality', pursued through intensified financial activity, industrial strategies that aim to foster economic growth, and technological innovation funded by Big Tech, the green transition advances the unique role that capitalism has long now attributed to technoscience and markets as the vehicle to human well-being. In 2024, many Silicon Valley companies dropped their net-zero pledges due to building new energy-intensive infrastructures (data centres, small nuclear plants) to support the growing demand for Artificial Intelligence (AI) models. At its most extreme, former Google CEO Eric Schmidt admitted that 'we are never going to meet the climate goals anyway', suggesting we should let AI 'solve the problem' (Niemeyer & Varanasi, 2024) as if it is a problem too great for human intelligence and its resolving requires immense energy and computing power. By intensifying the destruction of Earth's resources and exacerbating existing socio-economic inequalities between and within countries of the Global North and the Global South, the green transition further economises global environmental change, making it simply a frontier of financialisation and investment. It is a form of necropolitics (Mbembe, 2019) that dictates who must live and how to achieve 'climate neutrality'. Ultimately, it contributes to the depoliticisation of climate change by promoting a seemingly benign mega-project that humanity can universally embrace and pursue.

As an epistemic project, the green transition requires and is materialised through the homogenising control of knowledge production in the present so that ecological catastrophe can be averted in the future. Whereas in modernity, science was used to justify the imposition of a unified way to 'objectively measure' time, now it is used to justify the temporal regime of transition politics. As a political project, the green transition concerns the continuation of the vision of economic growth through the complete redesign of the equipment (labour and technology) necessary for its implementation. The problem with the green transition as an epistemic and political project is that it relies on the assumption that because there are universal needs, there is also a single way to address them and, therefore, a particular kind of knowledge ('a universal epistemic code', as Mignolo puts it) that can be employed to move us to a predefined and programmed future. As a result, it is not only 'nature and the universe [that are] subjected to time's arrow, or linear time' (Mignolo, 2011, p. 170) anymore; it is also the livelihoods and landscapes with which some communities live that are subjected to a logic that aims at a universal goal. In celebrating growth and development and masking injustice and destruction, this project erases or devalues certain forms of knowledge and local histories.

This reckoning with the knowledge systems and temporality orders that inform ecopolitics matters. An alternative to the unfolding transition politics would be a politics that offers space for plural temporalities and addresses epistemic and political injustices. This could include an understanding of time not linked to the utilitarian logic of economic power and a conceptualisation of time beyond the present time or what Indigenous scholar and community leader Ailton Krenan calls '*un tempo alem desse*'. Progress, the notion that we are going somewhere, is based on seeing time as an arrow – always going somewhere. As Krenak (2023, p. 36) argues, this is the basis of our deception. The value that a more pluralistic account of time brings is that it allows us to consider the re-creation of the world as always a possible event. We visit this argument more explicitly in the final section, where we engage with Krenak's proposition for the 'existence of the Earth as an active event, here and now'.

We contend that to envision more equitable futures on a climate-changed planet, it is essential to undo the homogenising temporal framework that underpins transition politics. This undoing cannot be realised without considering the mistakes of the past. In this section, we examined the temporal and historical dimensions of the green transition. This is a temporal notion that requires appreciation of the new conflict of temporalities opened by the ecological crisis. Whether formulated in terms of regimes of historicity or in geological time, anthropocenic time or even deep time, scholars point to the co-existence of multiple temporalities. In the next section, we turn to five imaginaries (technocapitalist, eco-authoritarian, ecosocialist, post-growth, and ecoanarchist) to study in detail their visions of transition and, therefore, of the future. While transition seems to describe a universal, widely shared vision, we show that each ecopolitical imaginary puts forward its version of transition pathways and transition endpoints.

3 Ecopolitical Imaginaries of Transition

Transition politics is not monolithic or uniform; it also does not fit within a single ideological frame. As discussed in this section, advocates of transition politics subscribe to different political and ideological viewpoints, envision disparate and often competing ecopolitical futures, and prioritise divergent and sometimes irreconcilable material arrangements. However, a shared dilemma is implicated in the various forms of transition politics: either transition to a decarbonised future or maintain the current fossil fuel-based societies, leading to ecological collapse. This dilemma functions not only as a form of political but also of emotional blackmail, as we further discuss in Section 4. The logic of anticipation or pre-emption is imbricated in transition politics in all its manifestations: the transition is a mechanism to pre-empt and control the future. As Anaïs Nony (2017, p. 102) notes:

> pre-emption is the appropriation of something before it emerges as a common opportunity. ... As a temporal logic, it refers to a situation where one opportunity is predicted to benefit some people over others.

The kind of anticipatory thinking (pre-emption) that informs transition politics relies on a linear understanding of temporality that, as discussed in the previous section, reduces ecological politics to a set of actions and policies that concern the future, for the benefit of some people over others. In the final section we discuss how an environmentally and socially just transition would be informed by multiple temporalities.

We contend that the assumptions underpinning and sustaining transition politics require a more systematic probing, both on the descriptive and the normative level. Although it is undeniable that we are amid an unfolding transition to a different ecological state (in a descriptive sense), the nuances and unequal outcomes of the attempt to manage this process must also be understood and interpreted in normative ways. In this section, we elaborate on the different ideological underpinnings of transition politics, assessing the conditions under which it takes an ambient Promethean character and preparing the ground for discussing its affective dimensions (Section 4). As discussed in Section 1, given the climatisation of politics, we propose that transition politics emerges as the overarching form of ecopolitics.[8] Nonetheless, when observed closer, as we endeavour in this section, transition politics takes various forms that may depart from hegemonic articulations of transition outlined in Section 2. In observing how the transition to low-carbon futures is envisioned today, we tease out how the imperative of transition justifies and legitimises policy priorities, technoscientific knowledge production, and intensified financialisation. The overarching point we make is that the idea of goal-oriented ecological politics and its associated preoccupation with anticipation and the future has created complacency about the state of the planet in the present; it has also led to erasing from public memory past mistakes that contributed to the current state of affairs while silencing the perspectives of those already marginalised in these debates. As Latour (2020, p. 426) observes, it is precisely ideas such as 'going somewhere', 'moving forward' or 'leaving the past behind' 'that 'cut one by one all the roots of reflexivity'. We concur and add that it is also these ideas – linked to 'progress' – that devastated the lives of Indigenous people and the nonhumans that that they consider part of their associated milieu. Counteracting these ideas is our purpose in the final section of this project.

Ecopolitical Imaginaries

In dissecting the various forms of transition politics, we employ the notion of imaginary. Following others who also argue for the crucial social role that imaginaries perform (Bottici, 2011; Castoriadis, 1997; Jasanoff & Kim, 2009; Taylor, 2004), we see them as valuable clusters of social meaning that inform expectations, affects, and desires, shaping practices and decisions. *Ecopolitical imaginaries* are collective visions for sustainable futures created through collaboration between different ecopolitical actors and express the ideas inscribed in people's imagination and material artefacts, from policies and institutions to technologies and novels, thus enabling meaningful interaction (Hatzisavvidou, 2024, 2025). Ecopolitical imaginaries are a useful heuristic to think about shared understandings of ecopolitical reality. They clarify how particular visions of the future gain prominence in public discourse and policy and how alternative viewpoints contest them. Though there are points of intersections and similarities, ecopolitical imaginaries differ from political ideologies. Like ideologies, they also work as 'mental frameworks' (Hall, 1998) that guide collective sense-making; however, imaginaries are not concrete ideational

---

[8] This is not to suggest that 'transition' exhausts ecological politics. For example, civil disobedience collective Désobéissance Ecolo Paris advocate for an ecology 'without transition'.

blocks, as different ideologies may inform them. Instead, they are clusters of co-produced social meaning that contain idealised visions for the future that evoke specific affects. This aspect of imaginaries is explored in more detail in Section 4.

Other researchers have previously identified specific imaginaries that organise social meaning and transformative action regarding climate change (Celermajer, 2021; Levy & Spicer, 2013; Machin, 2022). Following the approach of these researchers, we delineate imaginaries that emerge in academic texts, policy documents, and broader public discourse, which we have used as sources for our analysis. Rather than dissecting specific policies and plans, we outline the imaginaries that could implement them. Our discussion primarily concerns how different ecopolitical actors (policymakers, academics, activists, movements) envision the transition to sustainable futures. By attending to ecopolitical imaginaries, we consider the intersection of the political and the ecological, as well as the temporal and the affective. This approach allows us to move beyond the vague notion of 'transition', which is often used by political actors with varying and even competing ecopolitical projects. We explore the different political trajectories and visions associated with this notion. More specifically, we are interested in how the different imaginaries we identify affirm agency, temporality, technology, and envisioned outcomes; we are particularly interested in when and how the future becomes the raison d'être for damaging, extractive and exploitative forms of action in the present.

Ecopolitical imaginaries can play a vital role in responding to what Carl Death (2022, p. 444) calls 'the depoliticised, global, linear, and anthropocentric framing' of hegemonic manifestations of ecological politics. As our analysis clarifies, transition politics takes manifold forms; despite the current predominance of one particular imaginary, this is contested by other imaginaries. Alternative ecopolitical imaginaries do not only offer entry points for critique and departure from hegemonic framings; they also provide images and affective sources that help us see that it is 'always possible to picture things otherwise and to envisage alternative social relations' (Death, 2022, p. 437). In this sense, they are valuable sources for envisioning ecopolitical futures through action that unfolds in the present to shape the future; alternative ecopolitical imaginaries can function as compasses for navigating radically transformative possibilities. Importantly, as we discuss, they engage multifariously with temporality and the affective dimension of politics. This is why we find the analytical category of 'imaginaries' so central to our analysis: it allows us to consider the temporal and affective aspects of politics and the contestation that emerges among different ecopolitical agents.

In our discussion, we sketch five ecopolitical imaginaries through which transition politics gains cogency today: the predominant techno-capitalist and four emerging alternatives, eco-authoritarian, ecosocialist, post-growth, and eco-anarchist (Table 1).

Our taxonomical approach identify five imaginaries, it does not suggest they exhaust our ecopolitical condition or imagination. Reality is too complex and multi-layered to fit into neat analytical 'boxes'.[9] Table 1 is a way to offer an overview of how agency (who enacts and pursues the imaginary), temporality (what temporal order is employed), technology (how this is pursued), and envisioned outcomes for each of the five ecopolitical imaginaries we discuss. This does not capture all the possible ways that transition is envisioned today; instead, it demonstrates the diverse vantage points from which transition politics is supported and argued for and, therefore, to illustrate the significance of articulating and pursuing *a sixth ecopolitical imaginary* for a transition to just sustainable futures (which we attend to in Section 5). We purposefully analyse these imaginaries because we see them shaping the public debate (which unfolds on the political and academic levels) on the green transition today. By dissecting these divergent imaginaries, we highlight and attend to the diversity of transition politics without claiming that we offer an exhaustive analysis of ecopolitical imaginaries, past and present. Indeed, we would welcome future research that adds to the imaginaries we identify. We see this approach as a way to dispel the myth that environmental politics is a 'valence issue', namely an issue on which there is broad public agreement about desired policy outcomes and that is beyond contestation and disagreement. Our approach clarifies a second point: that environmental politics is inherently democratic or progressive. Indeed, as the following discussion shows, the climatisation of politics means abandoning our inclination to associate de facto and de jure green politics with left politics.

The Technocapitalist Imaginary

Industrial-scale renewable energy production plants. Deep ocean mining to extract critical minerals for the construction of necessary equipment. Global reforestation projects so that mitigation can be materialised at speed. Carbon

---

[9] Ecopolitical imaginaries are defined by the scale in which they emerge: they can be specific to certain localities or communities. In their ambitious exploratory study, Sovacool et al. (2020) have identified thirty-eight visions associated with seven different low-carbon innovations. While these visions are not ecopolitical imaginaries in their own right, they function as fragments that shape those imaginaries. Ecopolitical imaginaries are not simply produced from specific innovations (this would entail adopting a techno-determinist perspective) but they are conditioned by them.

Table 1 Ecopolitical imaginaries

Ecopolitical imaginary	Agency	Temporality	Technology	Envisioned outcome
Techno-capitalist	Markets, corporations, venture capitalists	Human time based on modernity and presentism	Geo-engineering, Carbon Capture and Storage (CCS), green energy, industrial-scale projects funded by private capital and requiring extractivism	Profitable green markets, privatisation of commons, consolidation of hierarchies
Eco-authoritarian	Elites, antidemocratic actors, traditional social structures	Human time based on modernity and *ancient regime*	Industrial-scale projects funded by private capital that rely on exploitation and extractivism	Racially homogenous communities come first, exclusion of immigrants, eugenics, conservation and preservation of natural landscape and patrimony/heritage
Ecosocialist	States, infrastructures	Modernity and geological time	State planning and public ownership for large scale-projects that require extractivism	Green new deal, ecological and social welfare state
Post-growth	Grassroots communities, collaborations between global North and global South farmers and workers	Presentism and geological time	Low-tech, circular economy, re-skilling (repairing, mending), decolonial technologies	Local production and consumption, post-development, *buen vivir*, convivial and frugal living, decolonised social relations
Eco-anarchist	Communities and anti-institutional actors	Presentism and geological time	Low-tech and circular economy	Federation, communalism, decolonised social relations

markets where harmful emissions are packaged into exchange and investment products. Technologies for geoengineering the climate that can alleviate the pressure to curb greenhouse gas emissions. Economic growth achieved through dematerialisation of production to address the increasing demand for 'green products'. The technocapitalist imaginary aspires to harness the power of unregulated markets, making (a particular manifestation of) ecology attractive to venture capitalists, green philanthropists, and Silicon Valley entrepreneurs alike. Even if the future is not necessarily greener in strict terms, it is essential that the transition to it can be financially more profitable and less risky. Projected as a series of exciting investment opportunities that will ensure that capitalism is still materially and ethically legitimate and accepted, this is the dominant or hegemonic ecopolitical imaginary today. Simultaneously, the green transition is a technological challenge that can be addressed through financial products that will ensure that the dominant economic system continues to run – the only change being the fuel: renewables in the place of fossil fuels. This phasist understanding of the transition relies on a linear view of time, whereby human history can be narrated as a series of successive stages.

This is the imaginary, for example, portrayed and advanced in the EU green industrial policy (European Commission, 2023), which exemplifies the shift to viewing the green transition as a matter of profitable investment.[10] Carbon pricing has been an essential element of this imaginary: if carbon prices are correct, markets and rational behaviours will adjust towards a sustainable future. There is no need for explicitly normative or prescriptive measures; economic actors will work towards green and innovative solutions (Durand & Keucheyan, 2024). However, the gap in the level of investment required and the inadequacy of carbon pricing created the need for green industrial policies that diversify the policy mix and lower market barriers (Jakob & Overland, 2024). The EU green industrial plan introduces programmes such as InvestEU, which aims to derisk green investment, a strategy also favoured by the World Bank, G20, fiscal hawks, and mainstream economists (Skyrman, 2024). Green derisking has the potential to accelerate decarbonisation by outsourcing it to private capital, while also derailing alternative pathways to decarbonisation (Gabor, 2023). The techno-capitalist transition is adaptationist, 'a quest not to avoid the change, but rather to minimise its consequences' (Felli, 2021, p. 10). In the

---

[10] There are voices within the EU that seek to part from, contest, or disrupt this imaginary. However, the failure of such voices to translate their positions into electoral results (see the performance of the European Green party in the 2024 elections) demonstrates precisely that the grip of the techno-capitalist imaginary allows very little space to alternative imaginaries in the arena of electoral politics.

technocapitalist imaginary, the green transition is an opportunity for enhancing private profitability.

Confronting the green transition as a technological challenge that can be addressed through green investment is another aspect of this imaginary. The concept of ambient Prometheanism captures this, the preoccupation with humanity's ability to confront the ecological crisis through optimistic but costly (and frequently unrealistic) technological interventions fuelled by intensified economisation while overlooking the social context within which these technologies and solutions emerge. The case of solar geoengineering is a point of relay: whereas in the past, such solutions were advanced mainly by conservative think tanks and politicians backed by the fossil fuel industry, today, they are promoted by coalitions of climate scientists, government agencies, environmental NGOs, and climate capital (Surprise & Sapinski, 2022). But behind the façade of grandiose innovative projects lies a deeply conservative spirit: its bearers see incremental, market-based decarbonisation as more palatable to technology capital (which now takes over the reins from the fossil capital). As Jesse Goldstein (2018) explains, clean technology entrepreneurship has fostered a vision of addressing climate change with new technologies that are hardly transformational. This new 'green spirit of capitalism' aims to 'save the planet by looking for 'non-disruptive disruptions' through technologies that deliver 'solutions' without changing much of what causes the underlying problems in the first place.

Oil and gas companies are among the most important actors in the world economy and determine the speed of the transition. They have little incentive to shift to renewable and green energy, while the shareholders' returns on investment are much higher on fossil fuels than on wind and solar power (Christophers, 2021). ExxonMobil was recently found to have largely exaggerated its plan for Carbon Capture and Storage (CCS), and it was found to be using its little investment in green technology to produce a greenwashing claim that drivers can 'fill up with less impact' (Webster, 2024). The UK chair of Esso noted that the investment in CCS would need a lot of public subsidies, showing that there was little economic advantage (apart from marketing) to deliver on the carbon capture plans. 'Subsidy' here is a euphemism for state support or what is now called 'de-risking' of renewables, giving large sums of money to fossil fuel companies to top up their profit (Christophers, 2021).

The shortcomings of the techno-capitalist imaginary already unfold in the present. Market-based solutions such as carbon pricing and green investment incentives have failed to achieve their primary goal of curbing global emissions, despite the optimism created when these solutions were introduced in 1997 with the Kyoto Protocol. The promised future never arrived, and mistakes conducted in the past do not inform judgement in the present. There is a constant deferral to future meetings, potential new markets, and generations-to-come to address the puzzles created by solutions that never worked effectively. The climate is managed using public management tools of efficiency, with phases, projects, and horizons. Although these solutions can yield incremental improvements and foster sustainable consumer behaviours, there is little evidence that they are the way to achieve the 'transformational' change that U.N. scientists say is necessary. These solutions paved the way for the further dispossession and exploitation of the Global South, as we discuss in Section 5. Focusing on competition, innovation, and the rationality of markets obliterates and underplays the criminal and unjust dimensions of the climate crisis for the poorest populations of the Earth. At the same time, the business-as-usual attitude of technocapitalism is mainly responsible for endemic climate anxiety, as we will discuss at length in the next section.

The Eco-authoritarian Imaginary

The urgency to transition to a green future creates space for the emergence of eco-authoritarian tendencies, sensibilities, and practices. The ideological links between environmental concerns and authoritarian ideas and governance are well documented. There is a long history of environmental and conservation movements endorsing xenophobic, nationalist, and racist ideas and practices (Bramwell, 1989; Taylor, 2016). Historically, authoritarian regimes developed environmental policies and strategies that served their social repression and political suppression agendas (Wilson, 2019). Today, we witness the emergence of far-right ecologies that draw invariably on fascism, conservatism, and reaction and bring together elements such as mysticism, organicism, autarky, authority, and nostalgia (Lubarda, 2020). Right-wing leaders, parties, and their supporters can be sceptical and even outright hostile to the climate agenda (Huber, 2020; Lockwood, 2018). Nonetheless, it is also true that far-right ecologies employ the trope of deep ecology on the supremacy of the Earth over humans as a vehicle to explicitly advocate for racial purity, migration control, and strict border policies (Roberts & Moore, 2022, pp. 104–108). Far-right futures manifest in racialised and immunitary forms, where the primary concern is racial purity, and the future is envisioned as under threat from external populations (Varco, 2023). Notwithstanding the empirical importance of these developments, here we are concerned with how the ecological transition is envisioned in the discourses, ideas, and practices of political actors who, in advancing the idea that humanity must transition to a more sustainable future, endorse authoritarian solutions and proposals. Specifically, we are interested in two strands of authoritarian transition politics: what we call anti-democratic climate politics and integral ecology.

One way transition politics takes an authoritarian turn is by expressing an antidemocratic sentiment inspired by the need for urgent action. This sentiment is shared by some proponents of 'deep ecology' (Devall & Sessions, 1985; Naess, 1973), the strand of ecology that prioritises nature's integrity over human well-being and that Murray Bookchin (1987) described as 'a vague, formless, often self-contradictory and invertebrate thing'. This vagueness and formlessness of deep ecology leave it open for appropriation by optimistic environmental activists, eco-reactionaries, and 'eco-miserabilists' (Thaler, 2024) who reject the false hopes of representative democracy and non-violent direct action. For the latter category, the need for rapid socio-ecological transformation calls for reconsidering the prioritisation of political values traditionally associated with democracy. If humanity is confronted with an existential threat, we need change at a pace and magnitude that renders socio-ecological visions attained through democratic political processes (either liberal or direct democracy) redundant or simply a luxury. Eco-authoritarians are highly critical of catastrophism; they see it either as a conspiracy or a distraction put forward by progressives (Lange, 2024). Hence, there is an emphasis on stigmatising green policies as 'punitive ecology' (Section 4). In other words, the central argument of this strand of eco-authoritarianism is that democracy is unable to resolve the challenges associated with the current ecological crisis. In its most extreme versions, this strand of the eco-authoritarian imaginary advances the idea that liberal democracy is indeed at the root of the problem.

Although the idea of an impending catastrophe has been central to ecology since the 1970s, it has been renewed and intensified since the publication of the IPCC Special Report in 2018. Resonating with earlier arguments on the Earth's natural limits, including its limited carrying capacity for population, deep or committed ecologists warn that this could lead even to the extinction of the human species (Bendell, 2018). This preoccupation with survival can lead to the endorsement of eco-authoritarian ideas and the questioning of the appropriateness of political principles such as freedom and justice given the state of the planet today. Theoretically, these arguments were famously developed by Shearman and Smith (2007), who argue that climate change exposes the limitations of liberal democracy and free market capitalism and advocates for an authoritarian green government guided by experts ('eco-elites'). Nonetheless, even if one accepts liberal democracy as the context of responding to climate change, in principle, liberalism and environmentalism are not incompatible and the extension of liberal values can lead to authoritarian responses (Brinn, 2021). Empirically, China's ecological civilisation project is implemented through careful planning and regulation to transition to a green energy system by 2060, a model branded as authoritarian environmentalism. This transition model entails centralising environmental governance, overlooking local needs and circumstances, resulting in high socioeconomic and ecological costs for extractive communities (Li & Shapiro, 2020; Lo, 2020). Crucially, the anti-democratic transition imaginary may blend in with the techno-capitalist outlined earlier; the distinguishing marker in the case of the authoritarian imaginary is that the transition entails the direct application of authoritarian political measures to ensure the viability of the desirable ecological outcomes. The imperative of transition requires a fully controlled, ordered, disciplined, and even violent governance model in the pursuit of an ecologically sound future. In this imaginary, the future becomes the raison d'être for oppression and is associated with sad affects like disappointment, fear, and pessimism (Thaler, 2024).

The second strand of the eco-authoritarian imaginary corresponds to the idea of a transition to what can be called *integral ecology*. Integral ecology is a term used by Pope Francis in his first *Laudato Si* (2015). Although Francis does not define integral ecology, he advances it as the framework for saving 'our common home'. Hinting an anti-capitalist sentiment (Löwy, 2015), in that it critiques the pursuit of economic growth at all costs, the ecopolitical imaginary advanced by Francis replaces the ecological transition with ecological conversion. Since environmental and social damage are linked, integral ecology can remedy both. As a result, integral ecology promotes a conservative ecopolitical arrangement, in which social relations are an extension of natural laws, and traditional techniques are fetishised, thus recovering well-rehearsed conservative arguments in the tradition of political thought.[11] Integral ecology retreats to an imaginary and glorified past of harmonious social and natural relations to inform its vision of the future. This produces a new conflict of temporalities between a glorified past to be sought and crisis-laden present. On this account, integral ecology shares ground with ecologies that seek to naturalise the social world in the name of interconnectedness, advocating for the exclusion of foreign people and cultures from 'native' populations and landscapes. It also shares ground with reactionary social movements that see LGBT+ people 'as a threat to "normal" society to which they supposedly do not belong' (Amery & Mondon, 2024). Their reactionary ideas are against all forms of biotechnology and interference with biological life, including abortion, IVF, and hormonal treatments. Building on fear and anxiety about social and environmental

---

[11] For instance, the far-right ideologue Alain de Benoist has appropriated the language of degrowth to advance a reactionary political project (Dubiau, 2023, pp. 96–100).

changes, integral ecology offers an essentialist organic imaginary that encompasses the human body, the family, and the natural environment, advocating a romantic vision for natural and social harmony that never existed.

The Eco-socialist Imaginary

Proponents of anti-capitalist arguments reject the possibility of 'greening' the current extractive and exploitative socio-economic system. Eco-socialists envision the green transition as an opportunity to transform existing production relations, break with the linear ideology of progress, and mobilise state and/or grassroots movement power to transition to more sustainable and more equitable futures (Foster et al., 2010; Löwy, 2002). Although the idea that capitalism is at the root of the unprecedented environmental changes facing humanity today is not new, it is an idea that was suppressed or appeased by the unifying rhetoric of sustainable development during the 1990s. Political developments such as the end of the Cold War, Third Way Politics, and the idea that history had ended contributed to the marginalisation of critiques of capitalism. The growing dissatisfaction with financialised capitalism during the late 2000s, the proliferation of extreme weather phenomena and ecological disasters, and the intensified outcry by the scientific community fostered the critique against the dominant capitalist system. The eco-socialist imaginary started to gain prominence among academic and activist communities, who explicitly linked the destructive nature of capitalism with the destruction of the natural environment. Despite the impressive growth of scholarship and advocacy for eco-socialist ideas and policies, this imaginary has remained primarily grounded in these domains, with little influence in policymaking. Although some of the discursive key markers of eco-socialism found their way to the dominant imaginary, including the notion of a Green New Deal, in reality, the implementation of these ideas quickly took a market-friendly turn. A notable example is the notion of a 'just transition' (Stevis, 2023). For many eco-socialists, the green transition must be 'just' to create a productive system that guarantees economic, social, and political equality (Velicu & Barca, 2020); for ecofeminists, this also means gender equality (Cohen & MacGregor, 2020). As Stefania Barca (2020, p. 50) explains, a 'just transition' that simply focuses on workers as the victims of the post-carbon transition 'reflects a masculinist and Western-centric bias ... focusing on blue-collar jobs in heavy industry and infrastructures as the only sectors worth defending and "greening", while downplaying the crucial contribution of agriculture, domestic and social reproduction work'.

The crux of this imaginary is that the very logic of capitalism is in opposition to biophysical reality, hence the need for a transition to a system that will be more ecologically sustainable and socially equitable. The future is here affirmed as a horizon of action in which the climatically necessary becomes the vehicle for the implementation of the socially desirable. For many proponents of this imaginary, humanity has not entered the Anthropocene, the Age of Humans, but the Capitalocene, the Age of Capital, an era first and foremost characterised by a certain political economy, a particular way of thinking about economic organisation and planning (Malm & Hornborg, 2014; Moore, 2015). Three main issues are raised against capitalism in this diverse scholarship. First is the ecological contradiction thesis, according to which capitalism operates in a way that undermines its background conditions. Nature is capitalism's condition and raw material: it uses nature for free both as a 'tap' to provide resources for production without replenishing them and a 'sink' to deposit waste. By doing so, capitalism essentially undermines its productive conditions (O'Connor, 1996), resulting in a series of ecological rifts (Foster, 2000; Malm, 2018). Second, the growth imperative inherent in capitalism entails that it is 'intrinsically geared to the maximum possible accumulation and throughput of matter and energy' (Foster, 2015) as a system. Natural limits are treated as barriers to be overcome, and, hence, capitalism tends to cross critical thresholds of environmental sustainability, causing needless and sometimes irrevocable destruction. Finally, the survival of capitalism requires and is supported by a culture of overconsumption, which causes excessive emissions and waste. The impacts of this culture are unequally distributed between the Global North and the Global South, with the latter bearing the brunt through the accumulation of harmful materials and substances. With the new competition for minerals and development of new mining sites, the colonial logic is central to the current extension of capital. As decolonial ecofeminist Francoise Verges (2017) argues, the new era is more precisely described as a 'racial Capitalocene'.

Behind these general points with which eco-socialists abide in various degrees lurk fundamental disagreements that make eco-socialism a multifarious ecopolitical imaginary. The transition to a new socio-ecological reality is envisioned through disparate and frequently competing technical and political pathways, which offer different responses regarding questions of agency, means to transition, and desired outcomes of the process. For socialists who embrace ecomodernist ideas, the green transition requires intense technological solutions deployed at an industrial scale by a workers' state. For example, Matthew Huber (2022) views climate change as a class war, identifying the roots of the problem with the activities of a particular class: capitalists and their profit from planet-destroying fossil fuel-based production. Huber advances a vision of working-class climate politics that would drive the green transition through public ownership, planning, and investment in industrial-scale productive systems, including clean energy infrastructure. Removing barriers posed by the capitalist pursuit of profit maximisation will allow the transition to an eco-socialist future. Similarly, Vettese and Pedergrass (2022) revive the socialist planning tradition and envision a planetary-scale ecological planning programme while problematising Promethean Marxism, nuclear power, carbon capture projects, and geoengineering. For socialist ecomodernists, the green transition requires class struggle, a shift in ways of production, and a Green New Deal that can ensure 'egalitarian green growth' (Pollin, 2015).

This imaginary of an eco-socialism that envisions planetary-scale ecological planning is not universally accepted among those who work towards systemic socio-economic changes. Barca's (2019) historical analysis of labour's eco-modernism unpacks the contradictions and fractures within this approach and counter-proposes a materialist ecofeminist understanding of post-industrial or reproductive labour and the ecological agency of working classes. Barca's argument illuminates the importance of considering the green transition to transform 'labour environmentalism into an antipatriarchal and anticolonial alliance between industrial and meta-industrial workers' (Barca, 2019, p. 233). This eco-feminist perspective is also shared by proponents of post-growth/post-development/degrowth imaginaries (see next paragraph, as well as Section 5). A different route to a radical approach to transition is offered by Andreas Malm, who advocates for an eco-socialist vision that bridges statist ecological planning and direct activism in the form of sabotage. The agent driving Malm's transition is a revolutionary subject: a movement against fossil capitalism that will 'institute a global prohibition of all new CO_2-emitting devices', starting with decommissioning and damaging them, thus making investing in this infrastructure unprofitable (Malm, 2021, pp. 67–69). Despite the strategic role of activists, Malm's eco-socialist imaginary culminates in the form of a state that operates as a wartime regime: an ecological war communism that will see through the transitional period away from fossil fuels. This period, Malm argues, does not have to be painful, in the same way that the imposed lockdowns during the COVID-19 pandemic were: it can be conducive to improving people's lives. As he explains, 'climate mitigation would never require people to become hermits in their homes. Convivial living would be conducive to that project' (Malm, 2020, p. 28). This is precisely where we need to consider and evaluate the role played by affects (positive and negative), which is a point we pick up in Section 4.

The Post-growth Imaginary

The rich anti-capitalist imaginary of transitioning away from the current fossil fuel-based socio-economic system is further diversified with the advancement of post-growth arguments. In the post-growth imaginary, it is not capitalist accumulation and exploitation that hinders an equitable green transition, but more specifically, the relentless pursuit of economic growth as an organising principle and social imperative. A key organising idea here is that a transition to sustainable futures requires abandoning the neoclassical economic logic and its methods (profit, accumulation, etc.), radically reducing the use of resources and energy, and creating a socio-economic system that will be based on collective democratic decision-making towards well-being, rather than economic growth (Kallis et al., 2020, p. 1; Schmelzer et al., 2022, p. 3). At the centre of the post-growth imaginary is the idea that the grip of growth on the current ecopolitical imagination is so firm that proposals that exclude or ignore it as a collective goal seem utopian or unrealistic. This is why a vital task for proponents of the post-growth imaginary is to decolonise the social imaginary from capitalism's pursuit of endless growth (Kallis & March, 2015). Whereas scholars and activists frequently employ the term 'degrowth' to precisely capture the need to dismantle the hegemony of growth (Kallis et al., 2020), 'post-growth' ('beyond growth' and even 'a-growth') offers a softer, non-prescriptive and less confrontational way to advance the vision of complete transformation and even provides a route towards focusing on the *process* and positive *outcomes* of transition, while remaining agnostic about the place of growth at the end of the transition (Raworth, 2017). The importance of this debate notwithstanding, here we affirm degrowth/post-growth as a normative concept that 'delineates the contours of a desirable, democratic transformation process, which focuses explicitly on analysing, criticising, and then overcoming growth dependencies' (Schmelzer et al., 2022, p. 27). We are not interested in repeating these conceptual debates (even though empirically they are essential) but in outlining what kind of transition beyond capitalism post-growth imaginaries advance.

The starting point of the post-growth imaginary is the idea that human well-being can be achieved within ecological limits or planetary boundaries – and that the current growth-obsessed economic system intentionally distorts this fact, creating unnecessary damage, waste, and violence. It is not only possible but also desirable to transition to a post-growth system of a non-growing (or steady-state) economy that can satisfy human needs and advance environmental sustainability, in socially equitable and politically democratic ways (Kallis et al., 2018; Schmelzer et al., 2022). A non-growth-oriented transition can be enabled and accelerated by reducing material throughput and energy demand, which helps to address climate change while removing pressure on other planetary boundaries (Hickel, 2020). A transition that does not aim at growth can also alleviate the effects of green colonialism, thus easing the geopolitical pressures exacerbated by dynamics of resource appropriation, addressing the global inequalities created by the unequal exchange between the Global North and the Global South, and opening pathways for decolonising transitions (Lang et al. 2024; Schmelzer et al. 2022). A current of post-growth imaginaries postulates that the safest way to materialise this transition is through economic and social planning (Durand et al., 2024; Hickel, 2020; Kallis et al., 2020; Schmelzer et al., 2022).

The transition to a well-being-oriented future within ecologically feasible boundaries requires drastic reductions of aggregate energy and unnecessary material use in the Global North. To maintain good lives for all, the post-growth imaginary requires changes in social provisions to secure human needs, including universal public services, economic democracy, and a shift in the understanding of 'progress' (Vogel et al., 2021). The equitable redistribution of resources between the Global North and the Global South also requires rethinking the role of technology and technological change in transitions and future arrangements. While large-scale high-tech production has a role in the post-growth transition imaginary, this production is focused on outputs that satisfy needs such as energy and public transport. A distinctive marker of this imaginary is that technology becomes a double question: first, a matter of *ownership* with downscaling of private ownership and investment towards public planning (Durand et al., 2024); second, a matter of definition or quality. The post-growth imaginary calls for embracing more *convivial* technologies, resonating with Ivan Illich's (1973) ideas on *convivial tools*: technologies characterised by relatedness, accessibility, adaptability, bio-interaction, and appropriateness (Vetter, 2018). The post-growth imaginary also calls for technological sovereignty, which allows for public control of the deployment of and reduction in monopolies and results in easing demand for materials in the Global South. Section 5 discusses how these ideas resonate with a decolonial and technodiverse transition imaginary. Focusing on care rather than economic growth entails envisioning alternative ways of prosperity, consumption, and happiness, which can result in less damaging ways of living, new forms of pleasure, and more viable and enjoyable futures (Soper, 2020).

The Eco-anarchist Imaginary

The ideological links between anarchist and ecological thought and practice run deep into the history of the environmental movement (Bookchin, 2005).

As John Barry (1999, p. 77) noted, for many green theorists, activists, and commentators, the 'sustainable society' in practice means stateless, self-governing communities plus solar power. This aptly summarises the eco-anarchist imaginary, which has had a resurgence, especially after the financial crisis of 2007–2009. Paradoxically, despite the relevance of eco-anarchist ideas and practices in theoretical and empirical terms today (Markoff et al., 2024), analytically, it is usually discussed alongside other imaginaries rather than as distinct approaches. In anticipating part of the discussion in Section 4 on affects and the role of political experiments such as the ZAD in Notre-Dame des Landes, we identify eco-anarchism as a distinct transition imaginary. For example, Bookchin's 'libertarian municipalism' (1991) and Trainer's 'simpler way' (2019) – presenting anarchist ecological transition frameworks – are frequently discussed as 'degrowth strategies'. These frameworks indeed resonate with degrowth propositions on the role of communities (as opposed to the state) in the transition and their emphasis on frugality, conviviality, solidarity, and care. Nonetheless, we believe that eco-anarchism should be treated as a separate imaginary. Here, we briefly focus on two elements of the eco-anarchist transition: the role of the alternative forms of political organisation and the place of violence in climate activism.

The ecological crisis presents an immense challenge in terms of political organisation, hence the constant need of the neoliberal state to adapt to emerging situations and to invent new instruments for governing a changing climate (Hatzisavvidou, 2020). A distinct marker of eco-anarchism is anti-statism, expressed through resisting the legitimacy of the state and envisioning alternative forms of self-government of empowered human communities organised confederally and pursuing harmonious co-existence with the natural world (Bookchin, 1991). Decentralised local communities operating through direct or participatory forms of collective decision-making serve as the agents of transition. In response to the privatisation of public spaces and services, these communities are implementing alternative political arrangements amidst the intensification of urbanisation and social isolation. Barcelona, Naples, Jackson, Belo Horizonte, and Grenoble are only a few of the places where residents and local authorities have decided that a more democratic, ethical, and just reality is possible and materialise forms of social and economic operation that are based on co-operation in sectors such as urban planning, housing, hospitality, and transport, which are also seen as promoting sustainability through the localisation of key public services (Thompson, 2020). The temporal emphasis on the present is a further marker of this imaginary: following the anarchist strategy of prefiguration (Leach, 2013), these political experiments allow for the unfolding of forms of relationship and modes of organisation that could be part of future ecopolitical arrangements.

Prefiguration is not the only strategy available to and employed by eco-anarchists. On 23 July 2017, two female environmental activists – Jessica Reznicek and Ruby Montoya – claimed responsibility for sabotaging the construction of the Dakota Access Pipeline (DAPL). As Lossin (2018) explains, property destruction or sabotage as a form of political militancy and resistance is 'a means of defending our shared environment'. The term 'sabotage', from the French expression to use the *sabot* (clog) to stop the machinery, has taken on a new political life; it is seen as a viable political strategy in the face of the climate crisis. Historically, sabotage belonged to the repertoire of political action in civil rights movements. Still, it is also associated with labour movements, as its main aim is to reduce production output. Therefore, the emphasis is on action rather than speech.[12] It is imaginative, diverse, and practical simultaneously, allowing every industry and worker solidarity to devise their forms of sabotage. In his much-discussed book on the topic, Malm (2021, p. 157) calls for nothing less than a call to arms, urging the climate movement to escalate its tactics and target 'the deformed kind of civilisation ... erected on the plinth of fossil capital ... and tear it down so that another form of civilisation can endure'. The recent criminalisation of environmental sabotage in different countries shows both a heightened threat from state institutions and an increasing effectiveness of eco-anarchism. This is because, as Lossin (2021, p. 95) points out, sabotage demystifies the capitalist mode of production and anticipates 'the moment in the future when property would be returned to its rightful owner and acted as if this moment had already arrived'. In this sense, sabotage is a form of 'pre-figurative expropriation' (Lossin, 2021, p. 95).

Prefiguration and sabotage are forms of unmediated action. In transition politics, sabotage is not aimed at realising the kind of sustainable society activists want to see; its prefigurative character is warning about the violence that is to come without giving it concrete forms. Nonetheless, both prefigurative politics and sabotage cultivate a relation to the future that envisions it as something that is or can be enacted in the present. Both prefiguration and sabotage are also mobilised or subsumed by non-anarchist activists, which brings our point home about the unavoidability of anarchism. Ecological prefigurative politics manifests as everyday sustainable practices unfolding on different scales, layers, and geographies, including agroecology, ecovillages, solidarity economy, worker-led production, energy and food sovereignty, free

---

[12] This point is made by Deleuze in an interview with Antonio Negri in 1992; the new form of sabotage according to Deleuze will have nothing to do with speech and communication as these have been thoroughly 'permeated by money'. 'We've got to hijack speech. Creating has always been something different from communicating. The key thing may be to create vacuoles of noncommunication, circuit breakers, so we can elude control' (Deleuze, 1997, p. 175).

software, deep just transitions informed by climate justice, and many others (Kothari et al., 2019; Schlosberg & Craven, 2022). Although forms of everyday environmentalism cannot be 'assigned to' or 'appropriated by' any specific ecopolitical imaginary, they demonstrate a strong desire from ordinary people to counter mainstream, top-down transition routes and adopt a form of prefigurative environmentalism.

4 The Joyful Transition

Advocates of transition politics forge imaginaries and mobilise people to apply them through various means, including policies, reports, white papers, academic outputs, and workshops with stakeholders and activists. This ecology of information is widely disseminated in public discourse via press outlets, websites, and educational programmes, aiming to shape behaviours, attitudes, and mindsets. But like all forms of politics, transition politics is not simply an attempt to shape cognitive understanding of the process of transitioning to post-carbon futures; it also contributes to organising and defining the affects that accompany this process. This is because all politics operates not only at the material (allocating resources) and cognitive (appealing to rationality) register but also at the register of sensibility (stirring affects and emotions). Despite Western philosophy's persistent tendency to treat cognition and affect as distinct regions, they should be understood as superpositions. As Jason Read (2016, pp. 104–105) notes:

> Political collectives are defined more by common structures of feeling than common notions or ideas. The central task of politics, any politics, is then to organise and define the affects.

Transition imaginaries are infused by and give cogency to different affects, which can either accelerate or slow down change, thereby influencing the temporal dynamics of politics and its experiences (as discussed in Section 2). By definition, affects are closely linked to transformation and change – increasing or decreasing the power to act.

In this section, we delve into the affective impact associated with the dominant transition imaginary and argue that transition politics can only achieve success if it fosters positive affects and in particular joyful ones. At the centre of our analysis lies the affect most commonly associated with climate change: what is widely known in psychiatry as 'eco-anxiety'. This affect transcends geographical boundaries, affecting young people in the Global North, displaced farmers in Uganda or Ethiopia for instance, and populations who fear losing their homes, jobs, and ways of life due to extreme weather conditions (Belay et al., 2017).

We propose that rather than simply focusing on ideas, values, and interests – which undoubtedly matter, as discussed earlier – we need to account for the role of affects in transition politics. This is a dimension often overlooked in debates in environmental politics, and this section addresses this blind spot. Elise Remling (2023) examines in productive ways the role of political fantasies mobilised in German climate adaptation policy to make adaptation discourses appealing. Remling calls to investigate this affective space that supplements the rational discourse of policymakers and other public actors. Interestingly, the influential sociologist of science Bruno Latour and his co-author Nikolaj Schultz (2022 par. 32) also identify the misalignment of affects as one of the challenges with ecopolitics, which hinders the development of 'unthinking habits'. Similarly Charbonnier (2018, p. 133) points out that 'ecological affects' are not yet adequately aligned with the political task at hand and work against politics itself. We argue that a decolonial imaginary requires the alignment of positive affects, thereby creating a common sense about transition and its material and affective objectives. Two key elements shape this common sense: reorganising attachments to technology and ecology and de-mythologising technology and nature. Technology will no longer be 'the big, spectacular, masculine high technologies of the rich white world' (Edgerton, 2008, p. xiv), and ecology will no longer be associated with punitive, sacrificial, or moralistic affects.[13]

Punitive Ecologies

Transition politics involves changing behaviours and attitudes, such as encouraging citizens to recycle, to cycle or walk instead of driving, to consume and pollute less and so on. However, the widely used methods employed to achieve this change are deemed 'punitive' by far-right groups in their anti-ecological politics. Far-right groups have invested in the terrain of ecology as fertile terrain for their reactionary agendas. They produce an 'inverted crisis', in which ecological policies (recycling, carbon taxes or low-emission zones) are deemed 'totalitarian', constraining and punitive, obscuring the material crisis of planetary warming (Zetkin Collective, 2024). These far-right groups exploit people's sense of exclusion from the public discourse and decision-making processes regarding ecological politics as well as the liberal hypocrisy of the fossil capitalist class. By labelling the green transition as 'punitive', far-right actors pretend to represent the people and assert that the ecological transition is too expensive and requires personal sacrifices (such as refraining from flying,

---

[13] We ought to consider technology and ecology as a nexus: the *technology-ecology nexus*. Only then can we critique the enhancement narrative of techno-optimists and the restrictive imaginary of ecology. For instance, the technology-ecology nexus shows that by augmenting the human body capacities (with robotics or AI), we also diminish or impoverish the planetary in other parts.

consuming meat, and watering the garden). This tactic can have detrimental effects on the social acceptability of necessary changes that are crucial for implementing any effective transition plan.

The case of the famous Yellow Vests' (*Gilets jaunes*) protests in France from 2018 to 2019 clearly illustrates this inverted crisis. This event marked the first collective rejection of the carbon tax, a measure often perceived as an essential element of transition plans. In France, this policy was voted on under the Hollande presidency (2012–2017) and introduced by Emmanuel Macron in 2018. It is based on neoclassical economics, cost-benefit analysis, and the 'polluter pays principle'. A carbon tax is one of the cornerstones of the energy transition since it suggests that setting the right price and charging individuals and companies for their carbon consumption can trigger large-scale behavioural changes and generate income for green investments and alternative energy sources. In opposition to this carbon tax and its top-down implementation, one of the widely mediatised slogans that dominated the initial phase of the protest read: 'elites talk about the end of the world when we talk about the end of the month' (Rassical 2018). As Ledoux (2018) observed, this slogan was framed in terms of temporal differences and varied experiences of time, expressing the sentiment that some individuals are more attuned to everyday life and a just-about-managing social condition than those preoccupied with distant concerns. Many Yellow Vest activists found this slogan inadequate to represent the movement, and its extensive mediatisation proved divisive and detrimental. As the climate movement gained momentum, Yellow Vest protesters adopted a revised slogan to 'end of the world, end of the month, same struggle'.

Another mechanism through which transition politics is advanced is through incentivisation, which involves using softer ways to produce behavioural change. Whether based on nudge theory or drawing from a more transparent and 'empowering' technique (such as 'boost'), these forms of psychological targeting consider individuals as consumers, thus reproducing the theory of possessive individualism.[14] Civil servants and government officials are widening further the gap between the public and the government by arranging the 'choice architecture' to influence behaviours and developing what Richard Thaler and Cass Sunstein (2008) refer to as 'libertarian paternalism'. For

---

[14] 'Consumers who are prone to addictive and compulsive behaviors or compulsive buying could be targeted by messages or interventions mitigating these adverse tendencies, for instance, by emphasizing the individual or environmental consequences of excessive or compulsive buying. Thus, data- and AI-driven marketing has to be leveraged for shifting consumers to more mindful and sustainable consumption behaviour. Thereby, AI in marketing provides a dual advantage for society at large by promoting societal and environmental well-being while preventing harm for consumers' (Hermann, 2023, p. 961).

instance, the EU-funded 'the NUDGE project' aims to promote energy efficiency in five EU member states by encouraging the adoption of smart meters and electric vehicles (EVs) or reducing energy consumption. The issue with this project is the focus on citizens as consumers and the use of techniques to profile individuals and employ basic rewarding mechanisms (such as discounts and bonuses as incentives) to encourage behavioural change. Similarly, in November 2020, the EU Commission released a New Consumer Agenda that seeks 'to empower consumers for the green transition with better information on products' sustainability and better protection against certain practices, such as greenwashing and early obsolescence' (EU Commission, 2020, p. 9). The press release for this new Agenda emphasises the European Commission's intention 'to empower consumers to become the driver of transition'.

One of the challenges with this type of psychological targeting is that it does not involve the public in finding solutions to the climate crisis or in finding relevant decision-making processes. To this extent, it deliberately tries to compete with advertising and marketing (which are also based on psychological models). However, this strategy proves to be self-defeating since for every pound spent on environmental marketing, there will be more spent by large corporations that encourage the public to buy more and thus consume more energy and materials (Goodwin, 2012). Therefore, psychological targeting is counter-productive as it works via diversion and stealth rather than using positive affects, as we want to propose in this section. It attempts to embed ecological transition in everyday life and focuses on incremental changes that, while necessary, are inadequate to achieve the required change.

Latour and Schultz (2022 par. 27) argue that the ecological movement will never be able to resist the label 'punitive ecology'. We disagree with this position and think there is potential to develop a new ecopolitical imaginary that undoes the far-right rhetoric of 'punitive ecology' and works towards a *beneficial ecology*. Labelling ecology 'punitive' discredits emerging initiatives and validates business-as-usual approaches. In this sense, it is a form of antipolitics, a powerful rhetoric from the far-right based on constructing an inverted crisis that seeks to undermine even soft ecopolitics. In this rhetoric, punitive ecology involves establishing new forms of taxation, norms, and obligations, but at the level of affects, punishment is associated with pain and suffering (Guibert, 2021). This logic of punishment – closely linked to techno-capitalist and eco-authoritarian ecopolitical imaginaries – deliberately exploits and distorts the conventional meaning of 'punishment'. In its everyday use, punishment refers to a privation of freedom by an authority to a single individual or a particular group due to wrongful actions. By definition, punishment cannot be applied to society in the same way (Wagner, 2023) as the unequal distribution of environmental risks and hazards demonstrates. A part of society is always subjected to more severe punishment than others. A punitive ecology, openly associated with the privation of freedom and being a killjoy, would never be able to unite individuals and groups that aspire to be part of transformative change. The actual privation of the world is organised by extractivist globalisation at the ontological level, separating humans from their being-in-the-world (Fischbach, 2011; Weintrobe, 2021) rather than by ecology and its advocates.

Surprisingly, Latour and Schultz persist in using the vocabulary of sacrifice and punitive ecology, giving legitimacy to a dangerous analytical and antipolitical category. They contrast their position with the modern passion for abundance and overcoming limits.[15] On the contrary, we do not think that it is contradictory to assert that the current ecological state of the planet affirms new limits to human action (Latour & Schultz, 2022 par. 28) while working towards a *beneficial ecology*. This role and place of limits in ecology is indeed fundamental (Kallis, 2019), and this reaffirmation of limits contributes to curbing ambient Prometheanism into a form of decolonial ecopolitics. However, there is confusion between two forms of limits: the limitations imposed on human action and the boundless resource of desire and affects. Desire and affect are, by definition, infinite and limitless.

Importantly, we argue that following Spinoza's politics of desire, we can give a new impetus to transition politics. Investing in field of desire and affects is productive for overcoming the pitfalls laid by far-right groups in their rhetoric of 'punitive ecology'. Ecopolitics will be about unleashing new forms of desire and joyful affects, rather than repressing them. Thus, following Spinoza, we argue that humans and possibly non-humans do not strive for something that is deemed good (and therefore accept being dispossessed or punished); instead, 'we judge something to be good because we strive for it, will it, want it, and desire it' (Spinoza, 1996 III, par. 9). Thus, *individuals and collectives will only participate in transition politics once they strive for it, not if they deem it good or legitimate*. Managers can inspire joy, love, and courage in workers by giving them a sense of self-realisation with cool workspaces and weekly socials with bean-roasting hipsters and craft brewers (Davies, 2015; Meiborg & van Tuinen, 2016, p. 16). There is a clear misalignment of affects ecology when we associate ecology with punishment and killjoy. At the same time, the workplace of major polluters and extractivist companies is linked to self-realisation and joy. This is not a glitch but part of the design of late capitalist society, to make exploitation and pain enjoyable while kinder and more sustainable ways of life seem

---

[15] This is what (Fressoz, 2012, p. 16) called 'disinhibition' in his work on technological risk: 'The word disinhibition condenses the two-step process: reflexivity and the paying of no heed, that of taking into consideration the danger and that of normalising it.'

unpleasant and taxing. Our problem is, therefore, how can we make the workplaces of extractivist companies sadder places to inhabit and simultaneously make socio-ecological movements more joyful?

Diagnosing Eco-anxiety and Searching for a New Psycho-collective Therapeutical Ecology

One of the recurring tropes in ecology is the exasperation with inaction, inertia, and passivity. This is partly due to the *immense gap* between the actions needed to create an ecological society and the current political plans. The failure of governments to address global climate change is contributing to new feelings of powerlessness, frustration, and despair, especially among young people. Whether climate policies openly call for sacrifices or use psychological targeting, climate anxiety is often ignored or underestimated. Transition politics requires rapid and collective action, and it will not be successful or even popular if it does not tackle front and centre the endemic problem of eco-anxiety. There will be no sustainable mode of living with nonhumans if eco-anxiety is not tackled.

In a widely publicised study, Caroline Hickman, Elizabeth Marks, and their colleagues surveyed 10,000 children and young people in 10 countries. They found that a staggering 59 per cent were very or extremely worried about climate change and 84 per cent were at least moderately concerned (Hickman et al., 2021). The common symptoms of eco-distress are sleeplessness, guilt, worry, fear, grief, and even shame (Hickman et al., 2021). Notably, eco-anxiety is increasingly given as a reason for not having children (Crist, 2020; McMullen & Dow, 2022). The emerging research on eco-anxiety is clear: it is a structural problem, and even when child psychiatrists make efforts to identify individual responses (Watts and Campbell, 2020), the main challenge remains at the national and even global levels. Indeed, the common perceptions expressed by young people in this important study relate to their 'perception of governments' responses to climate change' and the impact it has on 'their emotional and psychological reactions' (Hickman et al., 2021, p. e864). A recurring feeling expressed by the participants in this survey was the feeling of betrayal (Hickman et al., 2021, p. e870). This betrayal is not directly at previous generations but primarily at the failure of governments to mitigate climate change and to provide imagined futures. Given the immense scale of this phenomenon, governmental actions are perceived as superficial and cosmetic. Consequently, a crucial contributing factor to climate anxiety is the sense of exclusion from the decision-making process of the ecological transition.

The adverse affects of eco-anxiety are therefore produced not simply by the escalating and increasingly palpable global warming impacts but also by the dominant transition narratives and the governmental responses. Recent literature points to the necessity of developing promised-based or 'promissory legitimacy' that invests in the future and provides imagined futures in light of neoliberalism's exhausted inability to promise any better future (Beckert, 2020). Initiatives from international organisations and national governments, such as the national initiative Fossil-free Sweden (FFS), emphasised the role of promissory legitimacy by creating a new 'future dreamscape' to gain support for industrial decarbonisation (Brodén Gyberg & Lövbrand 2022). But these can also borrow from the same exhausted and obsolete modernist philosophies of history, forming 'a techno-optimistic extension of the fossil-intensive present' (Brodén Gyberg & Lövbrand 2022, p. 8). These planned imagined futures present hopeful, yet limited, attempts to engage with the affective dimensions of climate policies and transition politics.

Other civic actors, in particular charities and NGOs, engage more directly with eco-anxiety and present techniques or remedies to counter this new emotional epidemic. They offer support to young people to transform their negative emotions (eco-anxiety and grief) into positive ones – the terms 'action', 'agency' and 'activist' are often used here. For instance, the non-profit organisation Force of Nature aims to reach out to young people and provide 'Climate Anxiety to Climate Action' workshops, local self-organised 'climate cafés' in 46 countries and even #climateconfessions. 'Force of Nature aims to help young people shift out of anger, anxiety, frustration and despair; toward feelings of agency, determination, community and vision.' Similarly, Friends of the Earth published their own 'Top 10 tips to combat eco-anxiety with simple actions': spending time in nature; taking action; shopping second-hand; planning plant-based meals; cutting out single-use plastic; making space for wildlife; saving energy in your home; swapping flights for a UK vacation; cycling and walking short trips; switching to a green bank (Friends of the Earth, 2023). Both of these non-profit organisations play a crucial role in addressing the symptoms of eco-anxiety, but they do not engage with its underlying causes. Individuals who experience climate anxiety are more concerned about large-scale global consequences for human and nonhuman well-being than about their own personal well-being (Van Valkengoed & Steg, 2023).

The responses from Force of Nature and Friends of the Earth, however, operate at the (individual) level of emotions and not the (psycho-collective) level of affects (Brosch, 2021). The distinction between emotions and affects is useful here to delimit the individual from the collective domains as well as to make the affective order visible for political action. Building from affect theory, Read (2016, p. 105) clarifies this 'distinction between affect, understood as an impersonal intensity, and emotion, understood as a subjectivised and individuated feeling'.

Learning from this emotional epidemic, it becomes evident that transition politics deeply impacts our individual and social modes of being. It modifies our *conatus* (perseverance in our being). The orientation of the *conatus* comes from external relations; these encounters exert their own powers on our being and will, in part, determine the desire to act (Lordon, 2016, p. 17). We engage in actions only because we are compelled to do so by something, according to Spinoza's minimal definition of affect (1996, p. III): 'by affect I understand affections of the body by which the body's power of acting is increased or diminished, aided or restrained'. Ideas are linked to affects by augmenting or diminishing our power to act. One of the objectives of transition politics should be to increase our collective power to act in the face of the climate emergency, cause behavioural changes, and mobilise bodies. Spinoza provides valuable insights here, as joyful or sad affects have distinct consequences for our power to act and our desire to change.

Writing in the seventeenth century, Spinoza brings the place of the body (and bodies) in politics to the fore. Bodies are mobilised and are moved by affects. Transition politics produce sad affects that diminish our power to act by dissociating people from the climate issue and the planetary. The climate emergency does not challenge Spinoza's dictum (re-appropriated by Deleuze): 'no one has yet determined what the body can do' (Spinoza, 1996, p. III, par. 2). The potentials of the body do not yet have known limits. Human individuals and collectives are highly creative and capable of living in infinite ways.

Following the studies mentioned earlier, eco-anxiety as a mental health condition is spreading, and much more needs to be done at the political and social level to reduce it while 'ensuring that strategies to reduce climate anxiety do not trivialise or downplay the severity and urgency of climate change, or even demotivate people to engage in climate action' (van Valkengoed & Steg, 2023). This process can begin by exploring the political dimension of anxiety and channelling it towards more positive outcomes. Eco-anxiety can turn into anger or *ressentiment* if it is not listened to and cared for. It is essential to recognise the difference between eco-anxiety as an internalised phenomenon and its physical-material existence. We focus on the endemic phenomenon of eco-anxiety precisely because it concerns physical-material existence and their modes of life. We apply Spinoza's definition of negative and positive affects axiomatically – negative affects (such as eco-anxiety), therefore, diminish our capacity to act.

To be sure, we cannot separate so neatly positive and negative affects. For instance, Greta Thunberg's call 'I want you to panic!' is a legitimate and productive reaction to the failure of climate politics; its affects are less clear. The message draws from negative affects (panic and fear), but Greta Thunberg gave this speech aged sixteen years old, representing a hopeful and youthful voice, at the Davos World Economic Forum in January 2019. She aimed at policy change by disparaging the world leaders, speaking in the name of her generation and an imagined, more sustainable future. Whereas her interventions succeeded in evoking emotional responses among audiences, these were primarily negative emotions which may not necessarily lead publics to support climate action (Gan et al., 2024; Kenny et al., 2024).

Affects do not simply concern individual persons but the collective, and given the seriousness of climate anxiety today, we need to address this affect:

> Affect must be a way of grasping the abstractions [of contemporary capitalism] that determine individual and collective life, rather than a retreat into an interior free of them. (Read, 2016, p. 104).

Transition politics often overlooks the role of passions and affects in ecological politics, and yet, as we explained earlier following Spinoza, collective power does not come together individually and socially through the evocation of the good but through what we judge to be good (ecological transition) because we desire and strive for it.

Other philosophical traditions from the twentieth century, from Gilbert Simondon to Sara Ahmed, are useful in developing this affect theory of anxiety. Simondon argues that anxiety (as an emotion and an affect) poses a significant threat to the subject since it hinders the processes of individuation. Anxiety questions the very foundation of subjectivity, its sense of purpose, and its development. The traditional distinction between fear and anxiety lies in their relationship to an object: fear has an object, while anxiety is objectless (Ahmed, 2015, p. 64). Anxiety anticipates a 'threatening but vague event' (Rachman in Ahmed 2015, p. 64) such as the climate emergency. We can also apply Sara Ahmed's brilliant work (on the embodied politics of fear, race, and anxiety) to climate anxiety. Ahmed argues that the 'scene of a future injury works as a form of violence in the present', leading women to 'refuse to leave the enclosed spaces of home' (Ahmed, 2015, p. 64). Climate-anxious bodies – that are gendered and racialised, especially when looking at the global scale – are also shaped by this future injury. The neglectful state of affairs diminishes their power to act.

Climate-anxious individuals become the problem themselves, being blamed for feeling anxious. As Simondon suggests, 'in anxiety, the subject feels as if it exists as a problem posed to itself' (Simondon, 2020, p. 282). Anxiety also intensifies over time[16], by filling the subject in its entirety and preventing it from

---

[16] 'One thinks of more and more "things" to be anxious about; the detachment from a given object allows anxiety to accumulate through gathering more and more objects, until it overwhelms other possible affective relations to the world' (Ahmed, 2015, p. 66).

moving on to the next phase of being. It obstructs the process of individuation. 'In anxiety, the subject would like to resolve itself without going through the collective' (Simondon, 2020, p. 283). For Simondon, anxiety interrupts the processes of individuation that happen at the individual and collective levels to produce what he calls 'transindividuation'. Since the subject wants to continue its processes of individuation, it seeks 'a direct resolution [of anxiety] without mediation or delay ... [but it is also] an emotion without action' (Simondon, 2020, p. 283). However, this impatience paradoxically arises because subjects hope for a quick resolution of anxiety as a problem but are unable to act themselves, as anxiety immobilises the development of individual and collective being. Simondon even calls this subject a 'universal counter-subject': 'it is no longer localised, it is universalized according to a passive adhesion that makes it suffer' (Simondon, 2020, p. 283). To fully grasp the significance of Simondon's understanding of anxiety, it is crucial to consider his philosophical framework. For him, individuals are never fully constituted but are always individuating – an individual is a fully individuated subject as it would appear at the end of life. Emotions and affects, for Simondon, serve as vehicles (both psychological and social) to facilitate the individuation in relational and processual ways. Relational, since processes of individuation always take place in relation to a milieu.

Applying Simondon's ideas to the climate crisis, we notice how the climate regime creates a new associated milieu that problematises the subject's place in the world in a field of tensions. For Simondon, it is the labour of emotions to 'attempt to resolve the tension ... namely the initial and persistent incompatibility of the preindividual and individual that operates as the subject-milieu system' (Tucker, 2022, p. 10). Or again for Simondon, emotion is an embodied and social relation to the self and others, 'emotion signifies the need for action in the form of resolution' (Tucker, 2022, p. 10). This is where the labour of emotions takes place, and transition politics cannot afford to ignore. In this sense, the question of agency posed in Section 3 is clarified: the transindividual subject is affectively and, therefore, externally produced.

Tackling the two major challenges of contemporary politics (technology and ecology) requires acknowledging their psycho-social dimensions. Climate anxiety has become endemic and the effectiveness of governmental actions against climate change can be measured in relation to the levels of climate anxiety. Currently, it is only spreading and growing in uncontrollable ways. Interestingly, and we will delve deeper into this in Section 5, technological advancements have produced significant levels of anxiety, often coined as 'existential threat' or 'human extinction'. However, its real threat is much more from artificial selection and the capture of technology by elites. Thus, it is only by rethinking the relations between ecology and technology that feelings of loss, (de)privation, and anxiety can be addressed.

Local Experimentations and the Production of Joyful Affects

The challenge for transition politics is to produce joyful affects while actively dismantling some of the toxic economic, ecological, and affective structures that contributed to the formation of the Anthropocene. As we established in the previous section about the different transition imaginaries, there is no magical solution to the climate crisis. In the techno-capitalist imaginary, the myth of technofix and solutionism primarily exists to allow us to burn fossil fuels and accept the status quo. Technofix is an elite approach whose sole purpose is to state 'nothing to see here'. Ambient Prometheanism functions by suffocating the senses, blocking our ears, eyes, and mouths; it is a movement against epistemic justice (Section 2) and the diversity of technological inventions (Section 5). We propose that forms of local experimentation offer a possibility for producing the affects associated with a decolonial transition.

The Notre-Dame-des-Landes ZAD (*Zone à Défendre* or zone to be defended) was an acronym created by ecological activists and repurposed from the 1960s technocratic term *Zone d'Aménagement Différé* (Zone dedicated for a future development project). The project of building a new airport north of Nantes was first mentioned in 1967, and through waves of resistance, especially in 2012 and 2018, the €580 million airport project was eventually abandoned. In 2009, groups of activists first settled and began actively defending the land. The first collective wrote: 'to defend a territory, you have to inhabit it' (Fremeaux & Jordan, 2021, p. 56). The ZAD is currently inhabited by hundreds of activists, around 200–300 people, who reside in self-built and temporary dwellings. They have also developed creative agricultural experiments to care for the land. This land is neither wild nor farmed but has been co-created by humans and nonhumans for at least 200 years. This kind of land is known as *bocage*, due to its unique ecology:

> The *bocage* is the name for this increasingly rare type of landscape sculpted by two centuries of collective peasant life, planting hedges, digging ditches, tending pastureland and creating a checkerboard patchwork of small fields, crisscrossed by kilometers of hedgerows and little forests. Its network of ditches and ponds were designed to keep the water of the wetlands flowing and to stop erosion and flooding. Its polycultural mix of milking cows and fruit trees provided the conditions for a fairly autonomous closed-loop agriculture, with little need for imported resources and not much waste. (Fremeaux & Jordan, 2021, pp. 30–31)

In addition to the rich ecological history that Fremeaux and Jordan describe so powerfully, this territory is now the location of a village rich in activities and social relationships:

> With its bakeries, pirate radio station, tractor repair workshop, brewery, banqueting hall, medicinal herb gardens, a rap studio, dairy, vegetable plots, weekly newspaper, flour mill, library and even a surrealist lighthouse, the zad has become a concrete experiment in taking back control of everyday life. (zadforever.blog)

The ambivalence and ambiguity of local experimentations such as the ZADs ('zones to defend') stem from their avowed utopianism and their well-ordered way of life on occupied land. However, the starting point of activism is to be wary of romanticising social protests and falling for narcissism:

> If it's all 'yes', and if new forms of living are disconnected from the struggle against capitalism and forget who the enemy is (as is all too often the case in transition towns or schemes for a Green New Deal), they are easily folded into the existing system. . . .. Utopias without resistance become laboratories for the new spirit of capitalism. (Fremeaux & Jordan, 2021, p. 63)

We interpret these local experimentations not as models of utopian living, but as producers of joyful affects that help to connect the individual and the present to the collective and what is to come. While we may not live in the ZAD or even consider living in a communal setting like it, we are receivers of its images and positive affects. Joyful affects are viral and can travel far and wide. These local experimentations of ecological living witness and document alternative relationships between the world's different components and the attachments that they produce. They display different coordinates of the body as well as new attachments. Transition politics requires moving beyond the consciousness or awareness stage and towards recognising the entanglements of humans and nonhumans; the main challenge is *what we do about* these attachments.

One of the hurdles transition politics faces is the affective demands for the good life. Lauren Berlant's work is valuable here, as it explores why 'people stay attached to conventional good life fantasies' (Berlant, 2011, p. 2). These fantasies provide a false sense of comfort. A decolonial transition would require changing not merely relations between the state and the market but also 'the destruction and elaboration of fantasy in relation to what a life is and what a good life is' (Berlant et al., 2010, p. 3). This requires freeing subjects from the images and 'tableaux' of the good life – 'scenes of romantic life and upward to the desire for the political itself' (Berlant, 2011, p. 2). These images of the good life operate as a fantasy, leading to a 'wearing out of the subject' (Berlant, 2011, p. 28). It is not that 'images of rural revolt, with tear gas poisoning vegetable plots and youth being pulled out of trees' are more inspiring than Western fantasies of the good life; the issue lies in their ability to displace the affective economies of work, life, and commodified leisure. These images contribute to creating new eco-political imaginaries with distinct territorial coordinates. They do not advocate for a 'return to nature' but record new forms of life and attachment while exposing the brokenness of late capitalist social life. In this way, they can foster new attachments that generate joy rather than sadness and anxiety.

Returning to our discussion about the far-right's discourse on punitive ecologies, where the good life is associated with the fantasy of carbon-hungry activities (driving an SUV, eating meat or flying), adopting low-carbon behaviours can seem sacrificial and go against these fantasies. But as Berlant makes clear, these are fantasies that harm not just the planet but also families and communities. Therefore, it follows that joyful affects can never be deliberately produced; they happen accidentally, frictionally, and furtively. They are not devoid of negativity; this would be a misinterpretation of affect theory. Instead, they are nurtured in an environment of care and trust, not one of fear, punishment, and competition. The time of transition is a time of upheavals and radical openness in which new structures and equipment need to be built from the ruins. It is a time of optimism and opportunity but also a time in which traditional reference points are gone and 'people lose confidence in how to be together, uncertain about how to read each other and incompetent even to their desire' (Berlant, 2022, p. 33).

We read the images produced by social movements like the ZAD semiotically or aesthetically. They can be emitters of joyful affects or at least bring discord in sad regime of affects (eco-anxiety). Although this turn to the ecology of images might seem counterproductive and even a desperate attempt to find comfort, we believe their role is crucial when considering affects. We contend that these images and their associated joyful affects directly address the hegemonic eco-anxiety that we discussed earlier. They point to collective therapeutics that superpose the substantial financial investment from public powers required to combat the climate crisis effectively.

5 Technology for a Decolonial Transition

We started this project by diagnosing transition politics as a mechanism for organising societies, natures, affects, and resources in the present so that the Earth's atmosphere contains fewer greenhouse gases in the future. In this section, we build on our discussion of the various manifestations of transition politics and sketch the form a decolonial transition might take. In this transition, the role of technology is crucial, not only in the sense that a transition to sustainable futures will necessarily be technologically mediated but also in that a decolonial transition, by definition, also operates in a different relation to technology. We unpack and clarify technology's indisputable role in transitioning to just sustainable futures; in this section we turn to the ancient Greek myth of Prometheus and Epimetheus, which allows us to sharpen our understanding of technology and its relation to temporality. Starting from the premise that global environmental change is a technological issue through and through, with the naïve 'technophilia vs technophobia' debate (Brand & Fischer, 2013) now obsolete, we ask: What kind of technologies are worth making today? How do we evaluate their usefulness concerning our scientific knowledge and pressing socio-economic and environmental justice issues? Our aim here is to provide a series of reflections that could inform a decolonial transition imaginary. We draw on two bodies of scholarship: decolonial theory and practice emerging in the American continents (Escobar, Krawec, Krenak) and philosophy of technology, particularly the works of Bernard Stiegler and decolonial approaches to technology. The overarching argument is that a decolonial transition requires rethinking technology, its purpose, and new ways of living with it.

Amidst the unfolding technological and digital transition, considering technology's role in transition politics is to reckon with its place in the dominant cosmology; it is to reckon with the relation between technology and coloniality. This calls into attention the material aspect of the transition and the fact that there are large quantities of resources (sand, wood, metal, rare minerals, etc.) and labour power to extract and transform these resources into technical objects and infrastructures. Considering the nature of the current global capitalist system, 'technological development' requires asymmetric net flows of biophysical resources from poorer to richer countries, 'a net appropriation of materials, energy, land, and labour, while simultaneously generating a monetary surplus from those net appropriations' (Dorninger et al., 2021, p. 10). This unequal exchange is based on colonial histories and the multi-relational logic of extractivism, both frequently obscured from transition politics, particularly in the dominant technocapitalist imaginary. As Jason Hickel (2023) explains, the issue is not technology per se: the problem is the objectives of our economies and the structure of the economic system, which creates the imperative to 'transition out of capitalism'. We concur and expand: to imagine and materialise an exit from the current late-capitalist mode of production and consumption, we need to reimagine not only the role of technology in this transition but also its anthropological function. In this section, we assess what is understood by 'technology' in climate politics, who is seen as a legitimate driver of technology, and what the projected outcomes of this technologically mediated transition are.

A decolonial ecopolitical imaginary is already here, envisioned and enacted by those who resist the dominant ecopolitical paradigm and its extractive, exploitative character. Maintaining the instrumental and neutral view of technology – that it is simply a means to an end – and neglecting the cosmological and ontological aspects of technology circumvent this essential marker of all human societies (Almazán & Prádanos, 2024). Technology remains an analytical blind spot, or it is attributed what Hornborg (2019) calls a magical and uncritiqued quality. However, technology is an essential dimension of humanity; from the first tools like flints invented 3.3 million years ago to the latest Large Language Models (LLMs) like OpenAI's ChatGPT-4 or Google's Bard, technical objects have shaped human bodies, organs, and environments to the extent that we can study human evolution from a technological perspective. With the Anthropocene and the artificialisation of the Earth, 'natural selection makes way for artificial selection' (Stiegler, 2016, p. 13). A transition is already happening; it causes much devastation and pain in the name of technological progress. A richer understanding and use of technology is required to materialise a decolonial transition. This entails raising questions of agency and temporality concerning the transition.

The Wrong Kind of Technology?

Transition politics has led to a new arms race between world economies. The challenge to build a post-carbon world while keeping productivism, extractivism, and economic growth as the main engines of the economy has led to a new development model organised around the idea of decoupling growth from material use. Driven by the goal to lower emissions, green production has created an increasing consumer demand for green and smart technologies (such as electric cars, solar panels, and other green household gadgets powered by lithium batteries and operating through shiny silicon screens). As companies rush to secure the necessary materials for these products, extractivism takes a green form, whereby resource appropriation and extraction are taking place in the name of climate change mitigation (Bruna, 2023). Geopolitical dynamics change, and novel challenges emerge. For example, trade disputes between the United States and Europe with China are increasing, with the former accusing China of unfair competitive practices and misappropriation of foreign technology ('forced technology transfer') for geopolitical objectives (Alami & Dixon, 2020, p. 8). China's own historical experience of the two Opium Wars in the nineteenth century – where its defeat was perceived as the result of a lack of (Western) technology – resulted in the country's reconsidering its main strategic objectives in the twentieth century: technological development and modernisation are now seen as matters of the utmost importance (Hui, 2016, pp. 31–32).

Today, the situation is reversed; Western economies feel threatened by the Chinese economic model and try to defend their national companies, reinforcing a new economic nationalism focused on protecting (and subsidising) technology firms towards what Naomi Klein (2020) calls a 'Screen New Deal'.[17] Technology becomes 'the main agent of change' for a technology-focused transition 'towards a *more-than-human* or *beyond-human future*' (Taillandier, 2021) in its most transhumanist version.

While corporations and governments in the Global North take part in this costly and damaging race, it is the people who live in the territories where the minerals and materials necessary for this race are found that experience its most devastating effects. The pursuit of green growth and the required technological solutions has opened a new phase of dispossession of historically marginalised and exploited communities, maintaining and intensifying the logic of the colonial past and giving rise to novel forms of green colonialism with devastating effects on peoples and natures. As Lang et al. (2024, p. 5) note, it is impressive 'how the geographies where that appropriation takes place are imagined or represented as without people or conflict' and 'how certain landscapes, bodies and whole populations are rendered disposable', thus re-enacting forms of oppression – colonialism, racism, patriarchy – that have existed since the sixteenth century. The example of Morocco is particularly telling: the ongoing colonial environmental narrative labels territories historically managed by pastoralist tribes as empty and, therefore, as underutilised and available for investing in mammoth green energy projects (Hamouchene & Sandwell, 2023, p. 33). A green transition that relies heavily on 'climate-friendly', 'smart', and 'green technologies' that require vast amounts of natural resources cannot be materialised without the creation of more 'green sacrifice zones' (Zografos & Robbins, 2020) and therefore without dramatically shaping ecologies and further dispossessing the dispossessed. Such a transition cannot be just.

At the heart of this tragedy are universalising, Eurocentric understandings of technology that underpin the effort to govern the Earth's system. The notion of energy transition entered public discourse, first in the United States and then globally via the UN summits on climate change, as an issue of technological development. According to this narrative, an undifferentiated 'humanity' will be able to solve the problem of global carbon emissions when new and clean energy becomes cheap and easy to produce. Hence, the 1980s was the crucial decade when actions could have been taken to reduce carbon emissions – often narrated in classical tragic traits with 'heroes, villains and victims' (Caracciolo,

---

[17] Considering the history of Silicon Valley, it is not necessarily a 'new' deal but a continuation of the US subsidising of US research and development. See Mazzucato (2014).

2020; Rich, 2019). When negotiations fell through in 1989 and later, technological progress was mobilised as the solution to carbon emissions while postponing meaningful change. The green transition and technological progress are intrinsically linked and cannot be easily disentangled. Yet, it is important to note how technology is defined in discourses and practices of transition and progress. Industrial-scale technological projects that require vast amounts of materials dominate the hegemonic transition imaginary. In IPCC reports, climate mitigation and adaptation are presented as opportunities for innovation, with 'advanced industrialised nations' having the responsibility to 'transfer technologies' to the 'least developed countries'. We propose that this association of technology with a particular kind of knowledge and infrastructure lies at the heart of the transition puzzle.

Rethinking Technology

As we show in Section 2, poor understandings of technology underpin both the prevailing technocapitalist imaginary and the ecosocialist one; changing the economic system will not necessarily bring a 'just transition'. Developing critical ways of thinking about technology is thus inherent to thinking about the nature of transitions to sustainable futures. We take inspiration from the history of technical innovations (Edgerton, 2008; Fressoz, 2012); examining the social and political struggles at play in technological development allows for accounting for past mistakes and considering alternatives. We argue that the puzzle of transitions is exacerbated by the focus on 'big, spectacular, masculine high technologies of the rich white world' (Edgerton, 2008, p. xiv); our analysis offers a way of rethinking the relation between technology and ecology by returning to alternative ways of thinking about technology.

The question of the role of technology in ecopolitical transitions is frequently answered by alluding to the figure of Prometheus (Dillet & Hatzisavvidou, 2022; Keary, 2016, 2022). Although the myth of Prometheus and Epimetheus is central to Western thought and knowledge about technology, we note that Epimetheus's role in the myth is rarely accounted for. This omission is a convenient way to recount the myth because it allows for omitting the importance of acknowledging past mistakes. In the myth, when Epimetheus is tasked with distributing qualities to different species, he forgets to give any of these qualities to humans. To rectify this mistake, Prometheus steals fire from Zeus; to transfer it with sticks, he creates 'artificial fire', as opposed to Zeus's 'natural fire' (lightning) (Vernant, 2006, p. 479). Symbolising technology and human ingenuity, fire gives new powers and possibilities to humans but also brings new dangers.[18] Promethean thought remains popular today, synonymous with a defence of modernity and the continuing faith in human mastery over nature through science and technology (Keary, 2022, p. 71). At the same time, forgetting Epimetheus leads to a poor understanding of technology as instrumental and universal, disengaged from particular cosmologies and modes of being.

Stiegler (1998, p. 184) explains that this myth is a rich source for understanding technology because it calls into attention its links to heterogeneous qualities such as prostheticity, anticipation, mortality, forgetfulness, and reflexivity. The common Promethean understanding of technology views it in a simplistic way, associating it with 'the violence of man against *physis* [nature]' (Stiegler, 1998, p. 186). But as Stiegler's reading of the myth shows, technology is constitutive of the human condition.[19] Humanity arrived at the invention of speech, religion, and politics precisely because of Epimetheus's fault: his forgetting to give humans any qualities and the subsequent intervention from Prometheus. It is because Epimetheus committed a fault ('which amounts to witlessness, distractedness, imbecility, and idiocy') that necessitated the invention of technology, of prostheses and artifices. To forget the role of Epimetheus in this process is to commit a further fault: to forget the forgetful. It is also to forget the importance of the quality of reflexivity, of re-turning to what is always too late. But there is also tragic dimension to technology, as its 'ambiguous benefits turn finally against their beneficiaries' (Vernant in Stiegler, 1998, p. 189). The invention of prostheses has considerable consequences for humans; they will have a mode of existence of their own and will have to be managed as part of a larger ecology of things and life. The gift made to humanity is an intermediary, *suppléance* – that is both a temporary work as well as the act of standing for something.[20] The production of prostheses can only take place after Epimetheus's forgetting. There is no necessity to palliate or compensate for faults and lacks before the idiocy and mistake of *epimetheia* have taken place.

How can we understand the role of accidents, mistakes, and idiocy when considering technology in our present conjuncture, especially with regard to

---

[18] 'The gift made to humanity is not positive: it is there to compensate. Humanity is without qualities, without predestination: it must invent, realize, produce qualities, and nothing indicates that, once produced, these qualities will bring about humanity, that they will become its qualities; for they may rather become those of technics' (Stiegler, 1998, pp. 193–194).

[19] Stiegler follows the reading of historian J.-P. Vernant.

[20] 'Le don à l'homme n'est pas positif : il est une *suppléance*' (Stiegler, 1994, p. 201, emphasis added). In the English translation the term *suppléance* is translated as *compensation*, thus losing its polysemy.

the climate emergency? In Western thought, anticipation and planning have a positive meaning, as opposed to afterwardness and deferred thinking. We concur that this is a mistake in that it entails forgetting mistakes of the past and preventing acting on this forgetting. Today even Account Account Account — defenders of modernity who believe that technologies 'arise endogenously, i.e. in response to constraints on human progress, translated by the market into pricing signals that spur ingenuity' (1998, p. 184) – affirm that ecological transition will not happen automatically. However, it is the blind faith in human ingenuity, the lack of reflexivity on past mistakes, unintended consequences, and even idiocy that close off any discussion on the impossibility of mastering technics as well as on the constitutive aspect of technology. Technics 'must be given a temporal sense: anticipation, care, conservation, and so on, in a succession of mistakes' (Stiegler, 1998, p. 194). All technologies are transitional, and the ecological transition is necessarily technological.

Stiegler helps us think through the question of technology with regard to the time of transition. Considering the stage we are at (rapid environmental changes caused by certain human activities), as well as the imperative to transition to a radically different state of affairs, it is clear that the time of transition is that of 'after having done' (Baranzoni, 2017, p. 44), a regime of temporality that is based on afterthought and requires reckoning with the past. It is because of a series of mistakes in the past that the transition today is needed. The narrative of transition politics as manifests today can mask this essential role of the past. 'Mistakes' here are not to be interpreted as sporadic actions that were committed because of a lack of knowledge and resulted in unintended outcomes. Despite alluding to the pre-modern myth of Prometheus/Epimetheus and the series of faults that led to technology as the constitutive element of social coexistence, we contend that the errors that led to the climate crisis (and which created the necessity for the transition) have not always been accidental or unintentional. Climate colonialism is based on a larger project of imperialism and exploitation that was deeply intentional. Yet, the myth of Prometheus and Epimetheus (and Stiegler's analysis) allows us to think the temporal dimension of technology. When colonial faults and crimes were committed, decolonial technologies can palliate. Thus, we find the myth helpful in thinking about the impossibility of a transition without technology and the importance of considering the role of afterthought in designing just transitions. Although anticipation is essential when thinking about the future, as Stiegler (1998, p. 196) explains, considering life's open, undetermined, and improbable nature, it can only be an anticipation without predestination.

Decolonial Technology

Rethinking the role and place of technology in transitions to just sustainable futures and moving beyond simplistic understandings of technology opens the way for considering questions of time, agency, affect, and justice. Technology's modern association with innovation, progress, and economic growth prescribes a transition based on intensified economisation, ecological disaster, and social exploitation. A longer view of technological development shows that innovation is not central to that history when examining technology users and not discourses. In this respect, the work of historian of technology David Edgerton (2008: xii) is illuminating. He proposes to distinguish two perspectives on the history of technology: (1) an *innovation-centric* approach to technology, influenced mainly by economist Joseph Schumpeter's theory of innovation, and (2) a *use-centred* approach to technology as a more realistic perspective. The British historian prefers this latter approach to make visible non-Western, non-rich, non-white, and non-masculine technologies, what he aptly calls 'creole technologies' (Edgerton, 2007).[21] Discourses about technology often blind us to previous uses of technologies, the crafts, and skills amassed over time. New technologies only need to be marginally better to be adopted, and not massively better. It is due to marketing and consumer culture that these new technologies acquire the status they do. In reality, most technologies fail, especially 'innovative technologies'.

A use-centred analysis of technology is instrumental in making sense of the role of technology in transition imaginaries. As argued earlier, the human use of technologies is central in the planning of transition, but the emphasis on innovation obscures the human use of technologies as well as an evaluation of needs (Geels et al., 2017; Smil, 2010; Stephens, 2024).[22] To put it differently, innovation mostly focuses on shiny new tech funded by private equity rather than human (and nonhuman) needs and uses as well as the human (and nonhuman) costs. Some so-called 'green' technologies further intensify extractive and colonial practices, reshaping geopolitical conflicts, displacing populations and workers (and their families). The necessity to enact a new energy transition is not simply a technological or innovation problem; it requires thinking about social and economic inequalities, working conditions, social rights advocacy campaigns, as well as collective affects. The history of social conflicts teaches

---

[21] Our approach here follows Jennie C. Stephens's (2024) critique of technological optimism and its framing as patriarchal, white-male conceptions of privilege and power – what she calls 'climate isolationism'. The issue in her work is that she opposes too starkly 'energy democracy' and social change/social innovation from technology and does not engage with decolonial approaches to technology.

[22] Recently, there is a revival of interest in a politics of need. See Durand and Keucheyan (2024).

us that changing energy production also involves widespread local frictions, for instance, miners' strikes or neocolonial exploitative conditions in new mining practices. It has been shown that sites of current resource extraction have historically been 'plundered and deforested by systems of franchise, settler, and corporate colonialism' (Dawson & Gómez-Barris, 2022, p. 61). What is increasingly referred to as extractivism is both a material condition regarding land and territories and an epistemic logic that continues colonial histories. It is clear that a decolonial transition imaginary is conditioned on a different knowledge production system. As Bacevic (2021, p. 1214) argues, 'knowledge practices do not only reflect the legacy of these modes of exploitation, but directly benefit from them'. Thus, a decolonial transition imaginary connects the material and infrastructural side of knowledge production of climate solutions, technologies as well as other crafts and techniques.

The dominant transition imaginary (the technocapitalist one) advances the idea that decarbonisation of electricity is central to the transition mission, which is realised using technoscientific solutions. The shift in energy production is crucial in addressing the climate emergency. Yet, the solutions often presented (electric cars, carbon capture and storage, solar power, and nuclear) only focus on decarbonisation in electricity production and consumption, forgetting entirely about other industries that consume fossil fuels and produce carbon emissions. Part of the climatisation of politics is the shift of emphasis towards energy production and consumption. This fundamental shift in attention is positive, but it remains rooted in an uncritical perspective on technology. The recent research on the environmental costs of artificial intelligence and supercomputers shows the limits of technological change and calls for a reassessment of our assumption of scientific progress. While tech companies participate actively in colonial extraction, both in material and in knowledge production, they have also developed so-called 'climate tech' to provide their own technofixes to climate problems. Oil companies conducted misleading campaigns about their reduction of emissions to help sell their petrol and diesel. ExxonMobil/Esso have admitted that their investments in green technologies such as CCS were going nowhere, and that they would need a 'magic wand' to realise their climate pledges (Webster, 2024).

Recent efforts to develop decolonial approaches to technology share similar concerns with the hegemonic form of transition we examined in earlier sections. The authors of the 'AI Decolonial Manyfesto' (2021) point to the masculine, white, wealthy, and Western dimensions of AI technologies. AI tech companies also participate in the colonial matrix of power by extracting material resources and furthering structural inequalities. Beyond the cosmetic language of 'ethical AI' and inclusivity, the Manyfesto calls for community-based creations, 'stories and sensitive experience' to be included in the design and the production of these technical systems. Muldoon and Wu (2023, p. 80) argue that using the interpretative framework of the colonial matrix of power from decolonial theory does not mean to re-introduce 'over-simplified binaries which portray everything "Western" as bad and everything coming from the majority world as an emancipatory force for good'. Romanticising indigeneity is as problematic as the most Western-centric view on technology. Rather, this framework allows or calls us to examine in detail the socio-technical relations that are being created (in AI design, but also in the green transition work). For instance, in his critique of 'smart farming' that uses drones for crop spraying, Mobarak notes, 'solutions to many of today's key development challenges hinge not on creating new technologies and solutions, but in understanding why the poor do not adopt seemingly beneficial technologies that already exist'. The question of a use-centred analysis of technology introduced by Edgerton almost twenty years ago supports decolonial approaches to technology.

Central to the task of building a decolonial transition imaginary is first to challenge the kind of technologies that large Western corporations are promoting as the solution to climate change. As we have shown earlier, it is essential to develop a more complex understanding of technology by focusing on users, makers, and everyday adoption. Technologies are not value-free tools but carriers of values, contexts, and socio-technical uses (Winner, 1978). Again, developing a critical perspective on technology does not mean rejecting technologies or praising more non-technological ways of living. In this sense, decolonial approaches to technology share ground the heritage of Luddites who understood earlier than most that machines and technologies 'were undermining livelihoods and destroying their communities, and that targeting those machines was a valid strategy in their fight against it' (Mueller, 2021, p. 5).

To illustrate and contribute to the decolonial approaches to technology, we turn to two brief examples: (1) water harvesting in Rajasthan (2) the alliances created with beavers in North America. Of course, labelling these as 'decolonial technologies' is reductive and can even wrongly signal that these technologies are part of a decolonial resistance against the 'bad' Western influence. On the contrary, we use these examples here to illustrate our argument that a decolonial technology must be attuned to human and nonhuman assemblages, that there are ways of living with 'creole' (Edgerton, 2007) or 'mundane' (Sovacool, 2021) technologies. The nascent literature on decolonial technology is useful in demonstrating the stakes of the debate on the place of technology in the ecological transition. Crucially, the point is not to agree whether this or that technology is more or less 'decolonial', but to appreciate and recognise the decolonial project: to build material equipment and create techniques of existence against the logic of colonial technologies. Typically, colonial technologies are extractive, masculine, white, and developed from wealthy groups, resulting in further entrenching socio-economic inequalities. The two modest examples we employ (water harvesting in Rajasthan and alliances with beavers in North America) are meant to provide alternative conceptions of innovation and technology. In this sense, these examples are intended to be illustrative and evocative rather than definitive 'solutions' or part of a normative political project. We retain these two examples to emphasise the technological dimension of a possible decolonial transition imaginary and to complement debates about decolonial social innovation and designs (Escobar, 2015). While these examples are not the magical answer to all problems associated with a changing climate, they are decolonial precisely since they operate at the local level, quietly mending the unintended consequences created by large modernist projects such as damns or large water canals. The point about these decolonial technologies is not scalability, but the way they use local knowledge, enmeshing the human-nonhuman environment.

Droughts are one of the most significant challenges for many regions in the world. In Rajasthan, India, creative engineering was developed over centuries to 'harvest' rainwater. Indian water conservationist Anupam Mishra's (2001) work has shown that vernacular Rajasthani hydrological architecture developed over centuries is more adapted to the desertic climate and geology of Rajasthan than modern water systems made of modern materials (dams, concrete canals, pipes, etc.), not just technologically but also socially, aesthetically, and spiritually.[23] This ancient form of engineering functions with the activity of harvesting rain, dating back to at least the seventh century, and is still practised today. Three types of water are distinguished in the Rajasthani language: *palar pani* (rainwater), *patal pani* (groundwater), and *rejani pani* (fragmentary water). This last form *rejani* water is found dispersed and trapped right under the surface of the Earth, in the gypsum layer. It is often insufficient to fill pots and must be accumulated over time. As Mishra (2001, p. 17) explains, 'it is indeed a special art to construct a *kuin* [a miniature well] which will be able to collect this special *rejani* water. The *chejaro* who takes down a *kuin* having a circumference of 4 to 5 hands to a depth of 30 to 60–65 hands amply measures the skill and caution required'. Central to water harvesting techniques in Rajasthan is the collective construction and the maintenance of a water network of ponds (*kund*), small wells (*kuin*), step

---

[23] Similarly, Ajay Singh Chaudhary (2024) imagines an eco-modernism that builds from Islamic and Mughal vernacular passive cooling strategies with canals and fountains as alternative to the 'techno-mystical' and energy-intensive US model of air-conditioning.

wells (*baoli*), and tanks (*tanka*). These are created and maintained by local people drawing from ancestral knowledge and design, with no funding, state organisation, or private water companies. The social dimension of these vast engineering projects is guaranteed via generational, spiritual, and aesthetic attachments. Without the continuing devotion and respect of the people who use it, the water network would not have survived and continued to be used for centuries, and cities would have been abandoned due to the lack of water. The coupling of essential infrastructure and aesthetic/spiritual attachment is deeply unusual from a Western perspective. Mishra's pioneering work led to a revival of interest in water harvesting techniques by policymakers, governmental agencies, and NGOs in India and beyond (Levi, 2023, p. 133). This is part of a more general trend to include local communities in making technologies. In 2023, the editors of *Nature* called for more studies in the natural sciences on frugal technologies – which they define as a 'low-cost option for technology' that uses local material and knowledge (Anon, 2023: 8).

In this sense, these large architectural and engineering undertakings can be understood as a form of decolonial technology. The notion of cosmotechnics is also relevant here. Yuk Hui (2016, p. 19) defined cosmotechnics as 'the unification between cosmic order and the moral order through technical activities'. Hui's cosmotechnical project posits that multiple traditions of technological development exist. This is particularly significant in recognising the contingency of any technology and its associated modes of existence. For Hui, technology is far from universal and the diverse modes of existence in the world are co-constituted with local technologies (p. 289). The example of water harvesting in Rajasthan shows the imbrication between an engineered water network and a traditional way of life. Technology is not bound to capital: capitalism is a much more recent enterprise, and when we study the history of technical inventions, we find that the state and large private companies have captured them.

As previously argued, the contemporary discourse on technology is dominated by technoscience and resource-intensive gadgets, so decolonising technology also means getting rid of these biases. Again, Edgerton (2008) finds surprising the disappearance of horses in the standard history of technology (i.e. steam trains, cars, and rockets). Horses and donkeys were central to Western societies until the mid twentieth century and co-existed with cars, trains, and tractors. For instance, the German Army in 1945 had many more horses than Napoleon did in his invasion of the Russian Empire in 1812 (Edgerton, 2008, p. 34). Part of this invisibilisation can be explained by the fact that animals are not considered 'technology'; the foundational opposition between nature and culture/technology that constituted modernity prevails.

In Global South cultures, this opposition or 'great divide' is not always present. French anthropologist Baptiste Morizot (2023) emphasises this point by examining the ecological work of nonhumans, particularly beavers. By focusing almost entirely on human foresight, principles derived from modernity and Western ontology have not taken the alliances shaped between humans and nonhumans seriously (Morizot, 2023, p. 345). Beavers also transform the natural habitat, slowing down rivers, building dams, storing water in ponds, and spreading that water out in the landscape via channels (Fairfax & Whittle, 2020, p. 1). Beavers live to 'capture running water', rivers are their habitat, but they also despise the sound of running water (Morizot, 2023, p. 349). These neglected animals become allies to humans in their struggle against the increasing threats of wildfires, floods, and droughts. The colonial matrix of power has produced 'environmental amnesia' (Morizot, 2023, p. 353) of previous ecological arrangements; for instance, zones with beavers are three times more protected against wildfires than zones without beavers (Fairfax & Whittle, 2020). Therefore, this new multispecies alliance is based on remembering past ecological arrangements and landscapes, co-shaped during hundreds and even thousands of years, and acting on this forgetting. Emily Fairfax and Joe Wheaton's pioneering work in this domain has popularised the work of beaver dams. Hydrologist groups are now considering beaver dam-building activities a low-tech and low-cost strategy to build climate resilience. Restoration practitioners use strategies mimicking beaver dam activity and wood accumulation in riverscapes to help restore the interconnected floodplain, groundwater and channel habitats (Wheaton et al., 2019). The emphasis here is on process and not results, while the work of beavers alongside the river is ongoing. The restoration of riverscapes is not an exact science or a project that can ever be fully accomplished since it works with autonomous and regenerating activities (Morizot, 2023, p. 359). Crucially, the ecological investment in beaver dam activity is post-extractivist and thus decolonial: beavers are not considered a resource, and cannot be controlled or instrumentalised. Ecologists have developed fascinating strategies to negotiate and communicate with beavers. Alliances with beavers will remain imperfect since they rest on unpredictability and instability. This entanglement of human-nonhuman forces challenges Western ontology or cosmology, as we will discuss in the next paragraph.

As noted earlier, labelling these examples 'decolonial tech' is reductive. First, they often existed before the colonial matrix of power; and second, they do not necessarily best reflect the decolonial resistances at work in the world. Emerging decolonial approaches to technology can inform the decolonial transition imaginary we will now be sketching out.

A Decolonial Transition Imaginary

To counter the deliberate erasure of ways of thinking and living that differ from the dominant Eurocentric ways – the series of intentional 'mistakes' that resulted in the de-futuring of marginalised people and communities – we propose thinking with those who have been trying to uphold these modes of existence. This thinking-with can open ways for repairing and restoring damaged relations and natures by illuminating what a transition to just sustainable futures might look like. This is because transition politics in its current dominant manifestation is infused by a 'one world' Euro-centric and modern ontology, which comprises three key elements: 'an ontologically stark distinction between Nature and Culture, a dominant tendency to conceive difference (including the difference between Nature and Culture) in hierarchical terms, and a linear conception of time' (Blaser, 2009, p. 890). An imaginary for a decolonial – that is just for humans and more-than-humans alike – transition that breaks with these three damaging elements would require envisioning a different relation between the human and the more-than-human world; a de-hierarchisation of specific ways of living over others; and a conception of time that appreciates the role of the past in imagining the future. This is why the 'justice' underpinning the decolonial transition imaginary would address existing injustices and their underlying causes across different territories (local and global), layers (gender, race, class), and temporalities (past, present, and future). It would be intersectional, intergenerational, multispecies, and restorative. It would also be infused by a disposition of generosity, instead of exploitation. In this spirit, the previous discussion on decolonial technologies does not aim to appropriate these knowledge and practices, but to highlight and uplift their importance and contribution.

A transition imaginary that folds and advances these principles is already emerging. It is envisioned and defended by individuals embedded in historically and socially marginalised and impoverished communities that reject the association of the future with a rigidly predetermined end state and a trajectory to this state defined by the ideology of progress and economic growth at all costs. Against the dominant transition imaginary's fixation with the relentless pursuit of costly technological mega-projects that exhaust the Earth system and most of its inhabitants, the technologies discussed earlier support a decolonial, post-capitalist imaginary. Frugal, low-cost, and user-centred technologies allow for the confluence of practices that draw on multifarious ontologies and epistemologies; they also prevent and rectify the disconnection of the future from the past and the present that transition politics exacerbate. This is because technologies infused by an ethos that pursues the reduction of extraction, exploitation, and destruction are more attuned to the need to erase or at least ease the stark human–nature divide of modernity. Incorporating lessons from mistakes committed in the past, the aim of this imaginary is not a transition to a predetermined 'net zero' future, but 'a transition to an altogether different world' (Baranzoni, 2017, p. 44): a world where the interdependence of all living and non-living matter entails the need to co-exist in difference – and despite difference. The commonality, then, shared by the agents of this imaginary is the pursuit of living well on the planet, while ensuring the latter's habitability.

This double goal calls for rethinking the temporal regime of the transition. If the future is not already known or cannot be anticipated programmatically but remains open and to be explored along the way (Baschet, 2022), then the transition is the very process through which this opening and exploration takes place. As Jérôme Baschet (2022, pp. 198–202) explains, the Zapatista principle 'to walk while asking along the way' (*caminar preguntando*) captures this modality of operating; it also allows for bridging the future to the past, not in the sense of a sanitised or folklorised temporal modality, but as a source of support and creative impulse. Other historically oppressed communities share this appreciation of the past as indispensable in envisioning the future. For these 'ancestors of the future', the people who 'were first colonised when they took away [their] collective sense of a future' (Estes, 2019, p. xiv), unforgetting the past is central to creating collective futures. As Patty Krawec explains, this unforgetting entails 'reclaiming knowledge that is held in unspoken ways' (2022, p. 18). These knowledges include not only practices and technologies but also a connection and kinship to the world, an awareness of its interconnectedness, and hence of the process of its disappearance unfolding today in parallel to the unfolding of transition politics. Indigenous leaders and activists such as Ailton Krenak, who lament this disappearance and the dominant 'utilitarian existence that reduces everything to calculable skills', resources, and experiences, counter-propose the cosmic sense of life, a post-extractivist cosmovision (Krenak, 2020, p. 30) that views the Earth as a living organism and humans as one element within it. We build on this cosmovision and expand, adding: a decolonial transition requires a sense of attachment not only to Earth, but also to the low technologies that help to co-exist with the Earth, fostering a common understanding for living well that departs from the current destructive one. A decolonial transition can only be envisioned and materialised if these visions, knowledges, technologies, and kinships are acknowledged as parts of the transition process.

References

Ahmed, S. (2015). *The Cultural Politics of Emotions* (2nd ed.). Edinburgh University Press.

Alami, I., & Dixon, A. D. (2020). The strange geographies of the 'new' state capitalism. *Political Geography*, *82*, 102237. https://doi.org/10.1016/j.polgeo.2020.102237.

Almazán, A., & Prádanos, L. I. (2024). The political ecology of technology: A non-neutrality approach. *Environmental Values*, *33*(1), 3–9. https://doi.org/10.1177/09632719231209745.

Amery, F., & Mondon, A. (2024). Othering, peaking, populism and moral panics: The reactionary strategies of organised transphobia. *The Sociological Review*, *73*(3), 680–696. https://doi.org/10.1177/00380261241242283.

Anon. (2023). Frugal innovation: a low-cost option for technology. *Nature*, *624*, 8. https://doi.org/10.1038/d41586-023-03816-7.

Avelino, F. (2017). Power in sustainability transitions: Analysing power and (dis) empowerment in transformative change towards sustainability. *Environmental Policy and Governance*, *27*(6), 505–520.

Aykut, S. C., & Evrard, A. (2017). Une transition pour que rien ne change? Changement institutionnel et dépendance au sentier dans les « transitions énergétiques » en Allemagne et en France. *Revue internationale de politique comparée*, *24*(1), 17–49. Cairn.info. https://doi.org/10.3917/ripc.241.0017.

Aykut, S. C., & Maertens, L. (2021). The climatization of global politics: Introduction to the special issue. *International Politics*, *58*(4), 501–518. https://doi.org/10.1057/s41311-021-00325-0.

Bacevic, J. (2020). Unthinking knowledge production: From post-Covid to post-carbon futures. *Globalizations*, *18*(7), 1206–1218. https://doi.org/10.1080/14747731.2020.1807855.

Baranzoni, S. (2017). Anthropocenic times: Stratigraphy of a passage. *Azimuth*, *9*, 43–60.

Barca, S. (2019). Labour and the ecological crisis: The eco-modernist dilemma in western Marxism(s) (1970s–2000s). *Geoforum*, *98*, 226–235. https://doi.org/10.1016/j.geoforum.2017.07.011.

Barca, S. (2020). *Forces of Reproduction: Notes for a Counter-Hegemonic Anthropocene*. Cambridge University Press.

Barry, J. (1999). *Rethinking Green Politics: Nature, Virtue, and Progress*. Sage.

Baschet, J. (2022). Reopening the Future: Emerging Worlds and Novel Historical Futures. *History and Theory*, *61*(2), 183–208. https://doi.org/10.1111/hith.12263.

Basosi, D. (2020). Lost in transition: The world's energy past, present and future at the 1981 United Nations Conference on New and Renewable Sources of Energy. *Journal of Energy History*, *4*, 1–16.

Beckert, J. (2020). The exhausted futures of neoliberalism: From promissory legitimacy to social anomy. *Journal of Cultural Economy*, *13*(3), 318–330. https://doi.org/10.1080/17530350.2019.1574867.

Belay, Recha, J. W., & Woldeamanuel, T. (2017). Smallholder farmers' adaptation to climate change and determinants of their adaptation decisions in the Central Rift Valley of Ethiopia. *Agriculture and Food Security*, *6*, 1–35.

Bendell, J. (2018). Deep adaptation: A map for navigating climate tragedy. *IFLAS Occasional Paper 2*.

Berglund, O., Britton, J., Hatzisavvidou, S., Robbins, C., & Shackleton, D. (2023). Just transition in the post-pandemic city. *Local Environment*, 1–15. https://doi.org/10.1080/13549839.2023.2173732.

Berlant, L. (2011). *Cruel Optimism*. Duke University Press.

Berlant, L. (2022). *On the Inconvenience of Other People*. Duke University Press.

Berlant, L., Vischmidt, M., & Helms, G. (2010). Affect and the politics of austerity: An interview with Lauren Berlant. *Variant*, 3–6.

Blaser, M. (2009). Political Ontology: Cultural studies without 'cultures'? *Cultural Studies*, *23*(5–6), 873–896. https://doi.org/10.1080/09502380903208023.

Bonneuil, C., & Fressoz, J.-B. (2016). *The Shock of the Anthropocene: The Earth, History and Us*. Verso.

Bookchin, M. (1987). Social ecology versus deep ecology: A challenge for the ecology movement. In *Green Perspectives*: *Newsletter of the Green Program Project*.

Bookchin, M. (1991). *Libertarian Municipalism: An Overview*. The Anarchist Library. https://theanarchistlibrary.org/library/murray-bookchin-libertarian-municipalism-an-overview.

Bookchin, M. (2005). *The Ecology of Freedom: The Emergence and Dissolution of Hierarchy*. AK Press.

Bottici, C. (2011). Imaginal politics. *Thesis Eleven*, *106*(1), 56–72. https://doi.org/10.1177/0725513611407446.

Bramwell, A. (1989). *Ecology in the Twentieth Century: A History*. Yale University Press.

Bringel, B., & Svampa, M. (2023). The Decarbonisation Consensus. *Global Dialogue*, *13*(3), 28–31.

Brand, R., & Fischer, J. (2012). Overcoming the technophilia/technophobia split in environmental discourse. *Environmental Politics*, *22*(2), 235–254. https://doi.org/10.1080/09644016.2012.730264.

Brinn, G. (2021). The path down to green liberalism. *Environmental Politics*, *31*(4), 1–20. https://doi.org/10.1080/09644016.2021.1952798.

Brodén Gyberg, V., & Lövbrand, E. (2022). Catalyzing industrial decarbonization: The promissory legitimacy of fossil-free Sweden. *Oxford Open Climate Change*, *2*(1), kgac004. https://doi.org/10.1093/oxfclm/kgac004.

Brosch, T. (2021). Affect and emotions as drivers of climate change perception and action: A review. *Current Opinion in Behavioral Sciences*, *42*, 15–21. https://doi.org/10.1016/j.cobeha.2021.02.001.

Bruna, N. (2023). *The Rise of Green Extractivism: Extractivism, Rural Livelihoods and Accumulation in a Climate-Smart World*. Routledge.

Caracciolo, M. (2020). Negotiating Stories in the Anthropocene: The Case of Nathaniel Rich's Losing Earth. *Diegesis*, *9*(2), 16–33.

Carter, J. (1977). *Address to the Nation on Energy*. The American Presidency Project. https://www.presidency.ucsb.edu/documents/address-the-nation-energy.

Castoriadis, C. (1997). *The Imaginary Institution of Society* (K. Blamey, Trans.). MIT Press.

Celermajer, D. (2021). Grounded imaginaries: Transforming how we live in climate-changed futures. *Griffith Review*, *73*, 163–175.

Celermajer, D., Burke, A., Fishel, S., et al. (2025). *Institutionalising Multispecies Justice* (1st ed.). Cambridge University Press. https://doi.org/10.1017/9781009506243.

Charbonnier, P. (2018). Les Formes de l'affect écologiste: Des attachements à la critique. *Esprit*, *1–2*, 130–144.

Charbonnier, P. (2024, January 29). La Transition: Mission impossible? *Pierre Charbonnier Substack*. https://pierrecharbonnier.substack.com/p/la-transition-mission-impossible.

Christophers, B. (2021). Fossilised capital: Price and profit in the energy transition. *New Political Economy*, *27*(1), 146–159. https://doi.org/10.1080/13563467.2021.1926957.

Chu, A. (2024). New emissions data offers 'little encouragement' for green transition. *Financial Times*. www.ft.com/content/e9fdde92-cffa-4524-b626-3d26141a90f7.

Clary, M. Q. (2010). Transitions to democracy: Grand theory or grand approach? In H. J. Wiarda (Ed.), *Grand Theory and Ideology in the Social Sciences* (pp. 191–211). Palgrave.

Cohen, M., & MacGregor, S. (2020). *Towards a Feminist Green New Deal for the UK*. Women's Budget Group. https://pure.manchester.ac.uk/ws/portalfiles/portal/170845257/Cohen_and_MacGregor_Feminist_Green_New_Deal_2020.pdf.

Creti, A., Criqui, P., Derdevet, M., et al. (2024, January 22). Affirmer que la transition énergétique est impossible, c'est le meilleur moyen de ne jamais l'engager. *Le Monde*. www.lemonde.fr/idees/article/2024/01/22/affirmer-que-la-transition-energetique-est-impossible-c-est-le-meilleur-moyen-de-ne-jamais-l-engager_6212216_3232.html.

Crist, M. (2020). Is it OK to have a child. *London Review of Books*, 42. https://www.lrb.co.uk/the-paper/v42/n05/meehan-crist/is-it-ok-to-have-a-child.

Daggett, C. (2018). Petro-masculinity: Fossil fuels and authoritarian desire. *Millennium: Journal of International Studies*, *47*(1), 25–44. https://doi.org/10.1177/0305829818775817.

Danowski, D., & De Castro, E. V. (2017). *The Ends of the World*. Polity.

Davies, W. (2015). *The Happiness Industry: How the Government & Big Business Sold Us Wellbeing*. Verso.

Dawson, A., & Gómez-Barris, M. (2022). Energy states. *Social Text*, *40*(1), 39–67. https://doi.org/10.1215/01642472-9495103.

Death, C. (2022). Climate fiction, climate theory: Decolonising imaginations of global futures. *Millennium: Journal of International Studies*, *50*(2), 430–455. https://doi.org/10.1177/03058298211063926.

Deleuze, G. (1997). *Negotiations, 1972–1990* (M. Joughin, Trans.; p. 221 Pages). Columbia University Press.

Devall, B., & Sessions, G. (1985). *Deep Ecology: Living as If Nature Mattered*. Gibbs smith.

Dillet, B., & Hatzisavvidou, S. (2022). Beyond technofix: Thinking with Epimetheus in the anthropocene. *Contemporary Political Theory*, *21*(3), 351–372. https://doi.org/10.1057/s41296-021-00521-w.

Dorninger, C., Hornborg, A., Abson, D. J., et al. (2021). Global patterns of ecologically unequal exchange: Implications for sustainability in the 21st century. *Ecological Economics*, *179*, 106824. https://doi.org/10.1016/j.ecolecon.2020.106824.

Dubiau, A. (2023). *Écofascismes*. Grévis.

Durand, C., Hofferberth, E., & Schmelzer, M. (2024). Planning beyond growth: The case for economic democracy within ecological limits. *Journal of Cleaner Production*, *437*, 140351. https://doi.org/10.1016/j.jclepro.2023.140351.

Durand, C., & Keucheyan, R. (2024). *Comment Bifurquer: Les principes de la planification écologique*. Zones.

Earth System Governance Project. (2018). *Science and Implementation Plan of the Earth System Governance Project.* www.earthsystemgovernance.org/wp-content/uploads/2018/11/Earth-System-Governance-Science-Plan-2018.pdf.

Eckersley, R. (2021). Greening states and societies: From transitions to great transformations. *Environmental Politics, 30*(1–2), 245–265. https://doi.org/10.1080/09644016.2020.1810890.

Edgerton, D. (2007). Creole technologies and global histories: Rethinking how things travel in space and time. *History of Science and Technology Journal, 1*(1), 75–112.

Edgerton, D. (2008). *The Shock of the Old: Technology and Global History since 1900.* Profile Books.

Escobar, A. (2015). Degrowth, postdevelopment, and transitions: A preliminary conversation. *Sustainability Science, 10*(3), 451–462. https://doi.org/10.1007/s11625-015-0297-5.

Estes, N. (2019). *Our History is the Future.* Verso.

EU Commission. (2020). *New Consumer Agenda: Strengthening Consumer Resilience for Sustainable Recovery.* https://eur-lex.europa.eu/legal-content/EN/TXT/PDF/?uri=CELEX:52020DC0696.

European Commission. (2019). *Going Climate-Neutral by 2050.* https://op.europa.eu/en/publication-detail/-/publication/92f6d5bc-76bc-11e9-9f05-01aa75ed71a1.

European Commission. (2023). *A Green Deal Industrial Plan for the Net-Zero Age.* https://eur-lex.europa.eu/legal-content/EN/TXT/?uri=CELEX%3A52023DC0062.

Fairfax, E., & Whittle, A. (2020). Smokey the Beaver: Beaver-dammed riparian corridors stay green during wildfire throughout the western United States. *Ecological Applications, 30*(8), 1–8.

Felli, R. (2021). *The Great Adaptation: Climate, Capitalism and Catastrophe* (D. Broder, Trans.). Verso.

Fischbach, F. (2011). *La Privation du monde: Temps, espace et capital.* Vrin.

Foster, J. B. (2000). *Marx's Ecology: Materialism and Nature.* Monthly Review Press.

Foster, J. B. (2015). Marxism and Ecology: Common Fonts of a Great Transition. *Great Transition Initiative.* www.greattransition.org/publication/marxism-and-ecology.

Foster, J. B., Clark, B., & York, R. (2010). *The Ecological Rift: Capitalism's War with the Earth.* Monthly Review Press.

Fremeaux, I., & Jordan, J. (2021). *We Are 'Nature' Defending Itself Entangling Art, Activism and Autonomous Zones.* Pluto Books.

Fressoz, J.-B. (2012). *L'Apocalypse joyeuse: Une histoire du risque technologique*. Le Seuil.

Fressoz, J.-B. (2020). L'anthropocène est un 'accumulocène'. *Regards Croisés Sur l'économie, 26*, 31–40.

Fressoz, J.-B. (2022). La 'transition énergétique', de l'utopie atomique au déni climatique: États-Unis, 1945–1980. *Revue d'histoire Moderne & Contemporaine, 69*(2), 114–146.

Fressoz, J.-B. (2024). *Sans transition: Une nouvelle histoire de l'énergie*. Le Seuil.

Friends of the Earth. (2023). Top 10 tips to combat eco-anxiety with simple actions, *Friends of the Earth*, 16 January. https://friendsoftheearth.uk/climate/top-10-tips-combat-ecoanxiety-simple-actions.

Gabor, D. (2023). *The (European) Derisking State*. Preprint, SocArXiv. https://doi.org/10.31235/osf.io/hpbj2.

Gan, Y. S., Hayes, S., & Whitmarsh, L. (2024). The Greta Effect: Is there more public support for climate protesters who are young and female? *Environmental Science & Policy, 162*, 103924. https://doi.org/10.1016/j.envsci.2024.103924.

Geels, F. W., Sovacool, B. K., Schwanen, T., & Sorrell, S. (2017). Sociotechnical transitions for deep decarbonization. *Science, 357*, 1242–1244. https://doi.org/10.1126/science.aao3760.

Goldstein, J. (2018). *Planetary Improvement: Cleantech Entrepreneurship and the Contradictions of Green Capitalism*. MIT Press.

Goodwin, T. L. (2012). Why We Should Reject 'Nudge'. *Politics, 32*(2), 85–92.

Gramsci, A. (1971). *Selections from the Prison Notebooks of Antonio Gramsci*. Lawrence and Wishart.

Guibert, G. (2021). Is the ecological transition soluble in citizen democracy? *Futuribles, 445*(33–43). https://doi.org/10.3917/futur.445.0033.

Hall, S. (1988). Popular-democratic vs authoritarian populism: Two ways of taking democracy seriously. In *In The Hard Road to Renewal: Thatcherism and the Crisis of the Left* (pp. 123–149). Verso.

Hall, S. (1998). The great moving nowhere show. *Marxism Today, Special Issue*, 9–14.

Hamouchene, H., & Sandwell, K. (Eds.). (2023). *Dismantling Green Colonialism: Energy and Climate Justice in the Arab Region*. Pluto Press. https://openresearchlibrary.org/viewer/00f17fce-1221-4a50-bc6e-643d19f790f7.

Hanusch, F. (2024). *The Politics of Deep Time*. Cambridge University Press.

Haraway, D. (2015). Anthropocene, Capitalocene, Plantationocene, Chthulucene: Making Kin. *Environmental Humanities, 6*(1), 159–165. https://doi.org/10.1215/22011919-3615934.

Hartog, F. (2015). *Regimes of Historicity: Presentism and Experiences of Time* (S. Brown, Trans.). Columbia University Press.

Hartog, F. (2022). *Chronos: The West Confronts Time* (S. R. Gilbert, Trans.). Columbia University Press.

Hatzisavvidou, S. (2020). Inventing the environmental state: Neoliberal common sense and the limits to transformation. *Environmental Politics*, *29*(1), 96–114.

Hatzisavvidou, S. (2024). Envisioning ecopolitical futures: Reading climate fiction as political theory. *Futures*, *163*, 103456. https://doi.org/10.1016/j.futures.2024.103456.

Hatzisavvidou, S. (2025). Anthropocene imaginaries and the role of climate fiction. In A. Machin & M. L. J. Wissenburg (Eds.), *Handbook of Environmental Political Theory in the Anthropocene*. Edward Elgar.

Hermann, E. (2023). Psychological targeting: Nudge or boost to foster mindful and sustainable consumption? *AI & SOCIETY*, *38*(2), 961–962. https://doi.org/10.1007/s00146-022-01403-4.

Heron, K., & Dean, J. (2022). Climate Leninism and revolutionary transition. *Spectre*. https://spectrejournal.com/climate-leninism-and-revolutionary-transition/.

Hickel, J. (2020). What does degrowth mean? A few points of clarification. *Globalizations*, *18*(7), 1–7. https://doi.org/10.1080/14747731.2020.1812222.

Hickel, J. (2023). On technology and degrowth. *Monthly Review*, 44–50. https://doi.org/10.14452/MR-075-03-2023-07_3.

Hickman, C., Marks, E., Pihkala, P., et al. (2021). Climate anxiety in children and young people and their beliefs about government responses to climate change: A global survey. *The Lancet Planetary Health*, *5*(12), e863–e873. https://doi.org/10.1016/S2542-5196(21)00278-3.

Hopkins, R., & Astruc, L. (2017). *The Transition Starts Here, Now and together*. Actes Sud.

Hornborg, A. (2019). *Nature, Society, and Justice in the Anthropocene: Unraveling the Money-Energy-Technology Complex*. Cambridge University Press.

Huber, M. T. (2022). *Climate Change as Class War: Building Socialism on a Warming Planet*. Verso.

Huber, R. A. (2020). The role of populist attitudes in explaining climate skepticism and support for environmental protection. *Environmental Politics*, *29*(6), 959–982. https://doi.org/10.1080/09644016.2019.1708186.

Hui, Y. (2016). *The Question Concerning Technology in China: An Essay in Cosmotechnics*. Urbanomic.

Illich, I. (1973). *Tools for Conviviality*. Harper and Row.

International Energy Agency. (2022). *The Role of Critical Minerals in Clean Energy Transitions*. https://iea.blob.core.windows.net/assets/ffd2a83b-8c30-4e9d-980a-52b6d9a86fdc/TheRoleofCriticalMineralsinCleanEnergyTransitions.pdf.

IPCC. (2018). *Global Warming of 1.5o C*. http://report.ipcc.ch/sr15/pdf/sr15_spm_final.pdf.

Jakob, M., & Overland, I. (2024). Green industrial policy can strengthen carbon pricing but not replace it. *Energy Research & Social Science, 116*, 103669. https://doi.org/10.1016/j.erss.2024.103669.

Jasanoff, S., & Kim, S.-H. (2009). Containing the atom: Sociotechnical imaginaries and nuclear power in the United States and South Korea. *Minerva, 47*(2), 119–146. https://doi.org/10.1007/s11024-009-9124-4.

Kallis, G. (2019). *Limits: Why Malthus Was Wrong and Why Environmentalists Should Care*. Stanford University Press.

Kallis, G., V. Kostakis, S. Lange, B. Muraca, S. Paulson, and M. Schmelzer (2018). Research on degrowth. *Annual Review of Environment and Resources 14*(8), 1–26.

Kallis, G., & March, H. (2015). Imaginaries of hope: The utopianism of degrowth. *Annals of the Association of American Geographers, 105*(2), 360–368. https://doi.org/10.1080/00045608.2014.973803.

Kallis, G., Paulson, S., D'Alisa, G., & Demaria, F. (2020). *The Case for Degrowth*. Polity.

Kaplan, E. A. (2020). Is Climate-related pre-traumatic stress syndrome a real condition? *American Imago, 77*(1), 81–104.

Keary, M. (2016). The new Prometheans: Technological optimism in climate change mitigation modelling. *Environmental Values, 25*(1), 7–28. https://doi.org/10.3197/096327115X14497392134801.

Keary, M. (2022). A green theory of technological change: Ecologism and the case for technological scepticism. *Contemporary Political Theory, 22*(1), 70–93. https://doi.org/10.1057/s41296-021-00541-6.

Kenny, J., Geese, L., Jordan, A., & Lorenzoni, I. (2024). A framework for classifying climate change questions used in public opinion surveys. *Environmental Politics, 34*(6), 1114–1140. https://doi.org/10.1080/09644016.2024.2429264.

Knops, L. (2023). The fear we feel everyday: Affective temporalities in Fridays for future. *South Atlantic Quarterly, 122*(1), 203–214. https://doi.org/10.1215/00382876-10242784.

Köhler, J., Geels, F. W., Kern, F., et al. (2019). An agenda for sustainability transitions research: State of the art and future directions. *Environmental

Innovation and Societal Transitions, 31, 1–32. https://doi.org/10.1016/j.eist.2019.01.004.

Koselleck, R. (2018). *Sediments of Time: On Possible Histories*. Stanford University Press.

Kothari, A., Salleh, A., Escobar, A., Demaria, F., & Acosta, A. (Eds.). (2019). *Pluriverse: A Post-Development Dictionary*. Tulika Books.

Krawec, P. (2022). *Becoming Kin: An Indigenous Call to Unforgetting the Past and Reimagining Our Future*. Broadleaf Books.

Krenak, A. (2020). *Ideas to Postpone the End of the World*. House of Anansi Press.

Krenak, A. (2023). *Life is not Useful*. Polity.

Lang, M., Manahan, M. A., & Bringel, B. (Eds.). (2024). *The Geopolitics of Green Colonialism: Global Justice and Ecosocial Transitions*. Pluto Press.

Lange, E. L. (2024, May 4). Searching for the catastrophe signal. *Café Américain*. https://cafeamericainmag.com/searching-for-the-catastrophe-signal/.

Latour, B., & Chakrabarty, D. (2020). Conflicts of planetary proportion – A conversation. *Journal of the Philosophy of History*, 14(3), 419–454. https://doi.org/10.1163/18722636-12341450.

Latour, B., & Schultz, N. (2022). *On the Emergence of an Ecological Class: A Memo*. Polity.

Leach, D. (2013). Prefigurative politics. In D. A. Snow (Ed.), *The Wiley-Blackwell Encyclopedia of Social and Political Movements* (pp. 1002–1004). Blackwell.

Ledoux, S. (2018, December 4). Fin de mois ou fin du monde? Une défiance de temporalités. *Libération*.

Levi, R. (2023). The 'Sacred' Architecture of Anupam Mishra's Water-Culture. In A. Geva (Ed.), *Water and Sacred Architecture* (pp. 133–147). Routledge.

Levy, D. L., & Spicer, A. (2013). Contested imaginaries and the cultural political economy of climate change. *Organization*, 20(5), 659–678. https://doi.org/10.1177/1350508413489816.

Li, Y., & Shapiro, J. (2020). *China Goes Green: Coercive Environmentalism for a Troubled Planet*. Polity.

Lo, K. (2020). Ecological civilization, authoritarian environmentalism, and the eco-politics of extractive governance in China. *The Extractive Industries and Society*, 7(3), 1029–1035. https://doi.org/10.1016/j.exis.2020.06.017.

Lockwood, M. (2018). Right-wing populism and the climate change agenda: Exploring the linkages. *Environmental Politics*, 27(4), 712–732. https://doi.org/10.1080/09644016.2018.1458411.

Lordon, F. (2016). *Les Affects de la politique*. Le Seuil.

Lossin, R. H. (2018). Sabotage as environmental activism. *Public Seminar*. https://publicseminar.org/essays/sabotage-as-environmental-activism.

Lossin, R. H. (2021). No interests in common: Sabotage as structural analysis. *Journal for the Study of Radicalism*, *15*(1), 75–108. https://doi.org/10.14321/jstudradi.15.1.0075.

Löwy, M. (2002). From Marx to ecosocialism. *Capitalism Nature Socialism*, *13*(1), 121–133. https://doi.org/10.1080/104557502101245413.

Löwy, M. (2015). Laudato Si—The Pope's anti-systemic encyclical. *Monthly Review*, *67*(7), 50–54. https://doi.org/10.14452/MR-067-07-2015-11_4.

Lubarda, B. (2020). Beyond ecofascism? Far-Right Ecologism (FRE) as a framework for future inquiries. *Environmental Values*, *29*(6), 713–732.

Machin, A. (2022). Climates of democracy: Skeptical, rational, and radical imaginaries. *WIREs Climate Change*, *13*(4), 1–13. https://doi.org/10.1002/wcc.774.

Malhi, Y. (2017). The concept of the Anthropocene. *Annual Review of Environment and Resources*, *42*(1), 77–104. https://doi.org/10.1146/annurev-environ-102016-060854.

Malm, A. (2018). *The Progress of This Storm: Nature and Society in a Warming World*. Verso.

Malm, A. (2020). *Corona, Climate, Chronic Emergency: War Communism in the Twenty-first Century*. Verso.

Malm, A. (2021). *How to Blow up a Pipeline*. Verso.

Malm, A., & Hornborg, A. (2014). The geology of mankind? A critique of the Anthropocene narrative. *The Anthropocene Review*, *1*(1), 62–69. https://doi.org/10.1177/2053019613516291.

Mann, G., & Wainwright, J. (2018). *Climate Leviathan*. Verso.

Markoff, J., Lazar, H., Case, B. S., & Burridge, D. P. (2024). *The Anarchist Turn in Twenty-First Century Leftwing Activism*. Cambridge University Press.

Marquardt, J., & Delina, L. L. (2021). Making time, making politics: Problematizing temporality in energy and climate studies. *Energy Research & Social Science*, *76*. https://doi.org/10.1016/j.erss.2021.102073.

Mbembe, A. (2019). *Necropolitics*. Duke University Press.

McMullen, H., & Dow, K. (2022). Ringing the existential alarm: Exploring birthstrike for climate. *Medical Anthropology*, *41*(6–7), 659–673. https://doi.org/10.1080/01459740.2022.2083510.

Meiborg, C., & van Tuinen, S. (2016). Introduction. In *Deleuze and the Passions* (pp. 9–20). Punctum books.

Mignolo, W. D. (2011). *The Darker Side of Western Modernity: Global Futures, Decolonial Options*. Duke University Press.

Mihai, M., & Thaler, M. (2023). Environmental commemoration: Guiding principles and real-world cases. *Memory Studies*, *17*(6), 1378–1395. https://doi.org/10.1177/17506980231176037.

Mishra, A. (2001). *The Radiant Raindrops of Rajasthan*. Research Foundation for science, Technology and Ecology.

Moore, J. W. (2015). *Capitalism in the Web of Life: Ecology and the Accumulation of Capital*. Verso.

Morena, E., Stevis, D., Shelton, R., et al. (2018). *Mapping Just Transition(s) to a Low-Carbon World*. UNRISD. www.unrisd.org/jtrc-report2018.

Morizot, B. (2023). *L'Inexploré*. Wildproject.

Mueller, G. (2021). *Breaking Things at Work: The Luddites Are Right about Why You Hate Your Job*. Verso.

Muldoon, J., & Wu, B. A. (2023). Artificial intelligence in the colonial matrix of power. *Philosophy & Technology*, *36*(4), 80. https://doi.org/10.1007/s13347-023-00687-8.

Murphy, M. (2017). *The Economization of Life*. Duke University Press.

Naess, A. (1973). The shallow and the deep, long-range ecology movement. A summary- *Inquiry*, *16*(1–4), 95–100. https://doi.org/10.1080/00201747308601682.

Ndlovu-Gatsheni, S. J. (2021). The cognitive empire, politics of knowledge and African intellectual productions: Reflections on struggles for epistemic freedom and resurgence of decolonisation in the twenty-first century. *Third World Quarterly*, *42*(5), 882–901. https://doi.org/10.1080/01436597.2020.1775487.

Niemeyer, K., & Varanasi, L. (2024, October 6). Former Google CEO Eric Schmidt says ... *Business Insider*. www.businessinsider.com/eric-schmidt-google-ai-data-centers-energy-climate-goals-2024-10.

Nony, A. (2017). Anxiety in the society of preemption. On Gilbert Simondon and the noopolitics of the Milieu. *La Deleuziana*, *6*, 102–110.

Nordbland, J. (2021). On the Difference between Anthropocene and climate change temporalities. *Critical Inquiry*, *47*(2), 328–348.

North, P. (2010). Eco-localisation as a progressive response to peak oil and climate change: A sympathetic critique. *Geoforum*, *41*(4), 585–594.

O'Connor, J. (1996). The second contradiction of capitalism. In T. Bentos (Ed.), *The Greening of Marxism* (pp. 197–221). Guilford Press.

Paixão, C., & Meccarelli, M. (2021). *Comparing Transitions to Democracy: Law and Justice in South America and Europe*. Springer.

Pollin, R. (2015). *Greening the Global Economy*. MIT Press.

Pollock, J. G. A. (1989). *Politics, Language, and Time*. Chicago University Press.

Pope Francis. (2015). *On Care of Our Common Home.* http://w2.vatican.va/content/francesco/en/encyclicals/documents/papa-francesco_20150524_en ciclica-laudato-si.html.

Raworth, K. (2017). *Doughnut Economics: Seven Ways to think Like a 21st-century Economist.* Random House.

Read, J. (2016). The affective economy: Producing and consuming affects in Deleuze and Guattari. In C. Meiborg & S. vam Tuinen (Eds.), *Deleuze and the Passions* (pp. 103–124). Punctum books.

Remling, E. (2023). Exploring the affective dimension of climate adaptation discourse: Political fantasies in German adaptation policy. *EPC: Politics and Space, 41*(4), 714–734. https://doi.org/10.1177/23996544231154368.

Rérolle, R. (2018, November 24). 'Gilets jaunes': 'Les élites parlent de fin du monde, quand nous, on parle de fin du mois'. *Le Monde.*

Rich, N. (2019). *Losing Earth: The Decade We Could Have Stopped Climate Change.* Picador.

Rifkin, M. (2017). *Beyond Settler Time: Temporal Sovereignty and Indigenous Self-Determination.* Duke University Press.

Roberts, A., & Moore, S. (2022). *The Rise of Ecofascism: Climate Change and the Far Right.* Polity.

Rosenbloom, D., & Meadowcroft, J. (2022). Accelerating pathways to net zero: Governance strategies from transition studies and the transition accelerator. *Current Climate Change Reports, 8*(4), 104–114. https://doi.org/10.1007/s40641-022-00185-7.

Rosenbloom, D., Meadowcroft, J., & Cashore, B. (2019). Stability and climate policy? Harnessing insights on path dependence, policy feedback, and transition pathways. *Energy Research & Social Science, 50,* 168–178. https://doi.org/10.1016/j.erss.2018.12.009.

Schlosberg, D., & Craven, L. (2022). *Sustainable Materialism: Environmental Movements and the Politics of Everyday Life.* Oxford University Press.

Schmelzer, M., Vetter, A., & Vansintjan, A. (2022). *The Future is Degrowth.* Verso.

Shearman, D. J. C., & Smith, J. W. (2007). *The Climate Change Challenge and the Failure of Democracy.* Praeger.

Simon, Z. B., & Tamm, M. (2023). *The Fabric of Historical Time.* Cambridge University Press.

Simondon, G. (2020). *Individuation in Light of Notions of Form and Information* (T. Adkins, Trans.). University of Minnesota Press.

Skyrman, V. (2024). *Industrial Policy, Progressive Derisking, and the Financing of Europe's Green Transition.* ÖFSE Working Paper, No. 78. https://doi.org/10.60637/2024-WP78.

Smil, V. (2010). *Energy Transitions: Histories, Requirements, Prospects*. Praeger.

Smith, M., & Jones, R. (2015). From big society to small state: Conservatism and the privatisation of government. *British Politics*, *10*, 226–248. https://doi.org/10.1057/bp.2015.23.

Soper, K. (2020). *Post-growth Living: For an Alternative Hedonism*. Verso.

Sovacool, B. K. (2021). Who are the victims of low-carbon transitions? Towards a political ecology of climate change mitigation. *Energy Research & Social Science*, *73*, 101916. https://doi.org/10.1016/j.erss.2021.101916.

Sovacool, B. K., Bergman, N., Hopkins, D., et al. (2020). Imagining sustainable energy and mobility transitions: Valence, temporality, and radicalism in 38 visions of a low-carbon future. *Social Studies of Science*, *50*(4), 642–679. https://doi.org/10.1177/0306312720915283.

Spinoza, B. (1996). *Ethics*. Penguin.

Stephens, J. C. (2024). The dangers of masculine technological optimism: Why feminist, antiracist values are essential for social justice, economic justice, and climate justice. *Environmental Values*, *33*(1), 58–70. https://doi.org/10.1177/09632719231208752.

Stevis, D. (2023). *Just Transitions: Promise and Contestation*. Cambridge University Press.

Stevis, D., & Felli, R. (2020). Planetary just transition? How inclusive and how just? *Earth System Governance*, *6*, 100065. https://doi.org/10.1016/j.esg.2020.100065.

Stiegler, B. (1994). *La Technique et le temps, Vol. 1: La Faute à Épiméthée*. Galilée.

Stiegler, B. (1998). *Technics and Time, Vol. 1: The Fault of Epimetheus*. Stanford University Press.

Stiegler, B. (2016). *Automatic Society Volume 1: The Future of Work, trans. D. Ross. Cambridge*: *Polity* (D. Ross, Trans.). Polity.

Sultana, F. (2022). The unbearable heaviness of climate coloniality. *Political Geography*, *99*. https://doi.org/10.1016/j.polgeo.2022.102638.

Surprise, K., & Sapinski, J. (2022). Whose climate intervention? Solar geoengineering, fractions of capital, and hegemonic strategy. *Capital and Class*, 1–26. https://doi.org/10.1177/03098168221114386.

Taillandier, A. (2021). 'Staring into the singularity' and other posthuman tales: Transhumanist stories of future change. *History and Theory*, *60*(2), 215–233. https://doi.org/10.1111/hith.12203.

Taylor, C. (2004). *Modern Social Imaginaries*. Duke University Press.

Taylor, D. (2016). *The Rise of the American Conservation Movement: Power, Privilege, and Environmental Protection.* Duke University Press.

Thaler, M. (2024). Eco-miserabilism and radical hope: On the utopian vision of post-apocalyptic environmentalism. *American Political Science Review, 118*(1), 318–331. https://doi.org/10.1017/S000305542300031X.

Thaler, R. H., & Sunstein, C. R. (2008). *Nudge: Improving Decisions about Health, Wealth, and Happiness.* Yale University Press.

Thompson, M. (2020). What's so new about new municipalism? *Progress in Human Geography,* 030913252090948. https://doi.org/10.1177/0309132520909480.

Tooze, A. (2025, January 23). Trouble transitioning. *London Review of Books, 47*(1). www.lrb.co.uk/the-paper/v47/n01/adam-tooze/trouble-transitioning.

Trainer, T. (2019). Entering the era of limits and scarcity: The radical implications for social theory. *Journal of Political Ecology, 26*(1), 1–18. https://doi.org/10.2458/v26i1.23057.

Tucket, I. M. (2022). Simondon, emotion, and individuation: The tensions of psychological life in digital worlds. *Theory & Psychology, 32*(1) 3–18.

UN. (2023, December 13). *COP28 ends with call to 'transition away' from fossil fuels; UN's Guterres says phaseout is inevitable.* https://news.un.org/en/story/2023/12/1144742.

Urry, J. (2011). *Climate Change and Society.* Polity.

Van Valkengoed, A. M., & Steg, L. (2023). Climate anxiety is about more than just personal risks. *Nature Climate Change, 13*(7), 591–591. https://doi.org/10.1038/s41558-023-01718-0.

Varco, M. (2023). Volk utopia: Racial futures and ecological politics on the German far-right. *Geoforum,* 103823. https://doi.org/10.1016/j.geoforum.2023.103823.

Velicu, I., & Barca, S. (2020). The just transition and its work of inequality. *Sustainability: Science, Practice and Policy, 16*(1), 263–273. https://doi.org/10.1080/15487733.2020.1814585.

Vergès, F. (2017). Racial capitalocene. In G. T. Johnson & A. Lubin (Eds.). *Futures of Black Radicalism* (pp. 22–74). Verso.

Vernant, J.-P. (2006). *Myth and Thought among the Greeks* (J. Lloyd & J. Fort, Trans.). The MIT Press.

Vetter, A. (2018). The matrix of convivial technology – assessing technologies for degrowth. *Journal of Cleaner Production, 197,* 1778–1786. https://doi.org/10.1016/j.jclepro.2017.02.195.

Vettesse, T., & Pendergrass, D. (2022). *Half-Earth Socialism.* Verso.

Vogel, J., Steinberger, J. K., O'Neill, D. W., Lamb, W. F., & Krishnakumar, J. (2021). Socio-economic conditions for satisfying human needs at low energy use: An international analysis of social provisioning. *Global Environmental Change*, *69*, 102287. https://doi.org/10.1016/j.gloenvcha.2021.102287.

Wagner, T. (2023, January 21). Does punitive ecology make sense? *Bonpote*. https://bonpote.com/en/does-punitive-ecology-make-sense/.

Wakim, N. (2024, June 5). La France a-t-elle déjà réussi sa transition énergétique, comme le dit Jordan Bardella? *Le Monde*. www.lemonde.fr/chaleur-humaine/article/2024/06/05/la-france-a-t-elle-deja-reussi-sa-transition-energetique-comme-le-dit-jordan-bardella_6237476_6125299.html.

Watts, J., & Campbell, D. (2020). Half of child psychiatrists surveyed say patients have environment anxiety, *The Guardian*, 20 November. https://www.theguardian.com/society/2020/nov/20/half-of-child-psychiatrists-surveyed-say-patients-have-environment-anxiety.

WCED. (1987). *Our Common Future*. www.un-documents.net/our-common-future.pdf.

Webster, B. (2024, March 20). Oil giant admits it needs a 'magic wand' to keep green pledges. *OpenDemocracy*. https://www.opendemocracy.net/en/oil-firm-exxonmobil-greenwashing-carbon-capture-emissions-pledge.

Weintrobe, S. (2021). *Psychological Roots of the Climate Crisis: Neoliberal Exceptionalism and the Culture of Uncare*. Bloomsbury.

Wheaton, J. M., Bennett, S. N., Bouwes, N., Maestas J. D., and Shahverdian, S. M. (2019). *Low-Tech Process-Based Restoration of Riverscapes: Design Manual*. Utah State University Restoration Consortium.

Wilson, R. (2019). Authoritarian environmental governance: Insights from the past century. *Annals of the American Association of Geographers*, *109*(2), 314–323.

Winner, L. (1978). *Autonomous Technology: Technics-out-of-Control as a Theme in Political Thought*. MIT Press.

Zetkin Collective. (2024). The great driving right show. *Salvage 14*. https://salvage.zone/the-great-driving-right-show/.

Zografos, C., & Robbins, P. (2020). Green sacrifice zones, or why a green new deal cannot ignore the cost shifts of just transitions. *One Earth*, *3*(5), 543–546. https://doi.org/10.1016/j.oneear.2020.10.012.

Acknowledgements

We would like to thank many colleagues and friends who supported us during the research and writing of this Element: Aurelien Mondon, Fran Amery, George Newth, Peter Allen, David Moon, George Sotiropoulos, Mihaela Mihai, Danielle Cellermajer, James Martin, Amanda Machin, Cecilie Sachs Olsen, Carl Death, Paula Diehl, Oliver Marchart, Mathias Thaler, Corrado Fumagalli, Rossella De Bernardi, Alexandre Christoyannopoulos, Charles Devellennes, Declan Wiffen, Anaïs Nony, Sara Baranzoni, Alexander Wilson, Jeanne Etelain, Paolo Vignola, Emilia Marra.

Benoit: thank you Tara for your continuous encouragement, even in the hardest moments. For my side of the project, I was also very lucky to be accompanied by the boundless love of Nayab and Kavya, their everyday smiles and growing character.

Sophia: thank you, Miltos and Philippos, for being there and letting things be.

About the Authors

Sophia Hatzisavvidou
University of Bath
Sophia Hatzisavvidou is a Reader in Politics at the University of Bath (UK). She is the author of *Appearances of Ethos in Political Thought* (2016) and has published in *Contemporary Political Theory, Political Studies, and Environmental Politics*. Her work focuses on ecopolitical imaginaries, just transitions, and sustainable futures.

Benoit Dillet is a Senior Lecturer in Politics at the University of Bath (UK). He is the author of *The Political Space of Art* (with T. Puri) (2016) and the translator of Bernard Stiegler's *Philosophising by Accident* (2017). His work focuses on political theory of technology, affect theory and future climate imaginaries.

Cambridge Elements

Earth System Governance

Frank Biermann
Utrecht University

Frank Biermann is Research Professor of Global Sustainability Governance with the Copernicus Institute of Sustainable Development, Utrecht University, the Netherlands. He is the founding Chair of the Earth System Governance Project, a global transdisciplinary research network launched in 2009; and Editor-in-Chief of the new peer-reviewed journal *Earth System Governance* (Elsevier). In April 2018, he won a European Research Council Advanced Grant for a research program on the steering effects of the Sustainable Development Goals.

Aarti Gupta
Wageningen University

Aarti Gupta is Professor of Global Environmental Governance at Wageningen University, The Netherlands. She is Lead Faculty and a member of the Scientific Steering Committee of the Earth System Governance (ESG) Project and a Coordinating Lead Author of its 2018 Science and Implementation Plan. She is also principal investigator of the Dutch Research Council-funded TRANSGOV project on the Transformative Potential of Transparency in Climate Governance. She holds a PhD from Yale University in environmental studies.

Michael Mason
London School of Economics and Political Science (LSE)

Michael Mason is Associate Professor in the Department of Geography and Environment at the London School of Economics and Political Science (LSE). At LSE he is also Director of the Middle East Centre and an Associate of the Grantham Institute on Climate Change and the Environment. Alongside his academic research on environmental politics and governance, he has advised various governments and international organisations on environmental policy issues, including the European Commission, ICRC, NATO, the UK Government (FCDO), and UNDP.

About the Series

Linked with the Earth System Governance Project, this exciting new series will provide concise but authoritative studies of the governance of complex socio-ecological systems, written by world-leading scholars. Highly interdisciplinary in scope, the series will address governance processes and institutions at all levels of decision-making, from local to global, within a planetary perspective that seeks to align current institutions and governance systems with the fundamental 21st Century challenges of global environmental change and earth system transformations.

Elements in this series will present cutting edge scientific research, while also seeking to contribute innovative transformative ideas towards better governance. A key aim of the series is to present policy-relevant research that is of interest to both academics and policy-makers working on earth system governance.

More information about the Earth System Governance project can be found at: www.earthsystemgovernance.org.

Cambridge Elements

Earth System Governance

Elements in the Series

The Emergence of Geoengineering: How Knowledge Networks Form Governance Objects
Ina Möller

The Normative Foundations of International Climate Adaptation Finance
Romain Weikmans

Just Transitions: Promise and Contestation
Dimitris Stevis

A Green and Just Recovery from COVID-19?: Government Investment in the Energy Transition during the Pandemic
Kyla Tienhaara, Tom Moerenhout, Vanessa Corkal, Joachim Roth, Hannah Ascough, Jessica Herrera Betancur, Samantha Hussman, Jessica Oliver, Kabir Shahani and Tianna Tischbein

The Politics of Deep Time
Frederic Hanusch

Trade and the Environment: Drivers and Effects of Environmental Provisions in Trade Agreements
Clara Brandi and Jean-Frédéric Morin

Building Capabilities for Earth System Governance
Jochen Prantl, Ana Flávia Barros-Platiau, Cristina Yumie Aoki Inoue, Joana Castro Pereira, Thais Lemos Ribeiro and Eduardo Viola

Learning for Environmental Governance: Insights for a More Adaptive Future
Andrea K. Gerlak and Tanya Heikkila

Collaborative Ethnography of Global Environmental Governance: Concepts, Methods and Practices
Stefan C. Aykut, Max Braun and Simone Rödder

Institutionalising Multispecies Justice
Danielle Celermajer, Anthony Burke, Stefanie Fishel, Erin Fitz-Henry, Nicole Rogers, David Schlosberg and Christine Winter

Sustaining Development in Small Islands: Climate Change, Geopolitical Security, and the Permissive Liberal Order
Matthew Bishop, Rachid Bouhia, George Carter, Jack Corbett, Courtney Lindsay, Michelle Scobie and Emily Wilkinson

Transition Imaginaries: Contested Temporalities, Affective Politics, and Decolonial Technology
Benoit Dillet and Sophia Hatzisavvidou

A full series listing is available at www.cambridge.org/EESG

For EU product safety concerns, contact us at Calle de José Abascal, 56–1°, 28003 Madrid, Spain or eugpsr@cambridge.org.